STORIES OF THE CONSTELLATIONS

STORIES OF THE CONSTELLATIONS

Myths and Legends of the Night Skies

Kieron Connolly

SCHOLASTIC

www.scholastic.com

This edition published by Scholastic Inc., 557 Broadway, New York, NY 10012 by arrangement with Amber Books Ltd.

Distributed by Scholastic UK, Coventry, Warwickshire
Grolier International, Inc., Makati City, Philippines

1 2 3 4 5 6 7 8 9 10

ISBN: 978-0-545-65205-6

Editorial and design by
Amber Books Ltd
74–77 White Lion Street
London N1 9PF
United Kingdom
www.amberbooks.co.uk

Project Editor: Sarah Uttridge
Design: Zoë Mellors
Illustrators: The Art Agency (main artworks), Patrick Mulrey (star charts) © Amber Books Ltd

Printed in Shenzhen, China

Contents

Introduction

Imagine being in the desert at night, in a time before maps and bright cities, where the land is dark, but the stars are easy to see. Or being on a ship at sea, where there's only water and sky around you, but all night there's one star—Polaris—that will always show you which way is north. For thousands of years, a single star or groups of stars have been used to help sailors and travelers find their way.

But how did people make sense of the 3,000 stars that they could see in the night sky? They played a kind of connect-the-dots game. By joining up the stars into squares, lines, and curves, ancient people no longer saw a mass of random dots, but groupings of stars that they could recognize—three stars became Orion's Belt, seven stars became the Plow, five stars became the curl of a scorpion's tail. The night sky transformed itself into a sort of map where the

This is the constellation Cepheus, whose story can be found in the entries about his daughter Andromeda (page 16) and his wife Cassiopeia (page 38). With a square of stars topped by a triangle, Cepheus looks a little like the shape of a house. In the sky, he sits next to Cassiopeia. The top of his head—the point of the triangle—is near the North Star (Polaris).

human eye could pick out Leo, Gemini, or the Great Bear. And how better to remember these shapes, which we call constellations, than to give them stories—stories of heroes, gods, and monsters, and stories that helped to explain how the world was created.

Apart from being a map, the constellations were also a calendar. Without clocks, watches, or diaries, ancient farmers would use the first appearance of a particular constellation in the night sky as an indicator that it was time to plant their crops.

Today, we may not rely on the stars to find our way or to recognize the seasons, but we could if we really wanted to. After all, even the Apollo astronauts who went to the Moon in 1969 knew how to navigate by the stars just in case their instruments failed. So, look up!

This is the sea monster Cetus, who, like Cepheus, can be found in the stories about Andromeda (page 16) and Cassiopeia (page 38). Andromeda was about to be sacrificed to Cetus when the hero Perseus rescued her. Cetus is the fourth largest constellation in the night sky.

THE NIGHT SKY

When we look up at the night sky, we can see many, many stars. Each is a sphere of burning gas, just like the star that we know best—the Sun. Scientists think that the Sun was created in a supernova—an eruption of energy— about 4,000 million years ago. Fragments from the explosion became the planets of our Solar System, including the Earth. The Sun is the nearest star to Earth, but it is still 93 million miles (150 million km) away. Traveling at a speed of 35,000 miles per hour (56,000 km/h), it would take a spaceship from Earth 111 days to reach the Sun.

This, however, is tiny in terms of the whole Universe. The Sun is the center of our Solar System, but that is just

The star map on the right shows what can be seen all year round in the northern part of the Northern Hemisphere—north of Philadelphia, Pennsylvania, or Madrid, Spain. It's the area shaded red on the globe below. The Big Dipper, probably the first pattern

that you will learn to find, is toward the top of the star map. Drawing a line from the Big Dipper's star Merak to Dubhe and continuing it leads directly to the North Star.

On the opposite side of the map from the Big Dipper is the distinctive "W" shape of the constellation Cassiopeia.

THE SKY ABOVE THE NORTH POLE

part of the galaxy we're in—the Milky Way. Holding about 400 billion stars, the Milky Way is 100,000 light years across. And how far is a light year, you might ask. It's the distance light travels in one Earth year. This distance is almost 6 trillion miles (10 trillion km). That's 6,000 billion miles (10,000 billion km).

If you could see the Milky Way from above, it would look like a disk with a spiral structure, rotating slowly. But if you left our galaxy, you would travel through space where there were no stars until you reached another galaxy, of which there are billions scattered across the Universe. Galaxies are like islands of stars in a vast ocean of space.

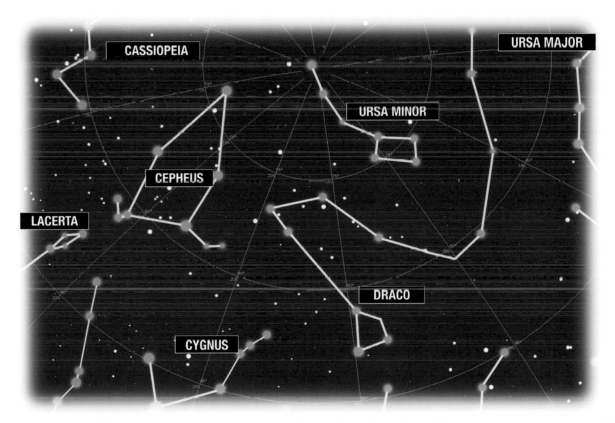

At the top of the map you can see the North Star (Polaris) marking the tip of the tail of the Little Bear (Ursa Minor). Beneath the Little Bear is the snaky shape of the dragon Draco. To the left of the Little Bear is Cepheus, Cassiopeia's husband, whose constellation is shaped like a house.

THE SPEED OF LIGHT

It takes eight minutes for light from the Sun to reach the Earth. That means that we see the Sun as it was eight minutes ago. Light from the dwarf planet Pluto takes four hours to reach us because it's 3 billion miles (5 billion km) away. And it takes four years for light from the star Alpha Centauri to reach Earth. When we look at Alpha Centauri, which we can find in the constellation Centaurus, we're seeing the star as it was four years ago. So, we say that Alpha Centauri is four light years away. When we use a telescope to look at stars that we can't see with the naked eye, it's a little like using a time machine—the telescope takes us back to what the star looked like minutes, hours, or years ago.

The stars in the part of sky shown on the right are visible in the evening from September to December in both the Northern and Southern Hemispheres, but not at the extremes. At the top of the map can be seen the edge of the constellation Cassiopeia and her daughter Andromeda.
  Beneath Andromeda is Pegasus. The four stars that make up the Square of Pegasus are fairly bright stars.

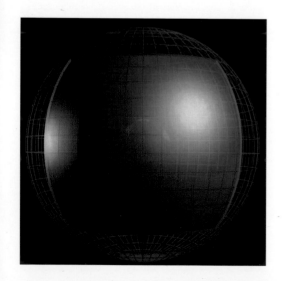

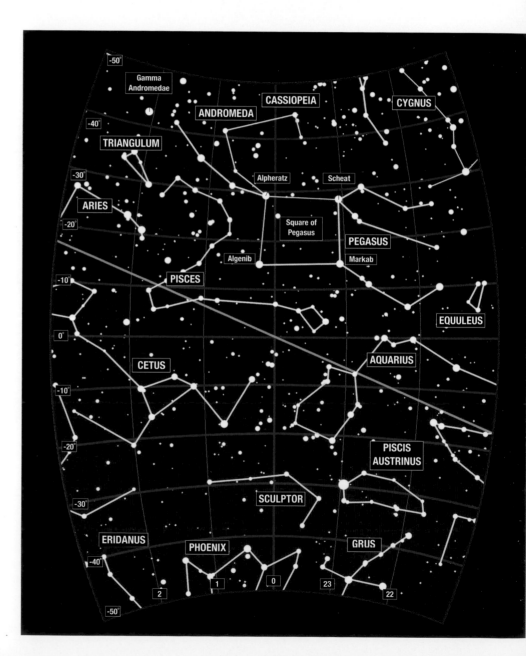

NORTHERN FALL SKIES

THE SPINNING TOP

The Earth is a bit like a spinning top that is about to topple—it does not rotate upright, but at a slight angle. As it is always rotating at a slight angle, the side directed toward the Sun will receive more sunlight. In December, the Southern Hemisphere is directed more toward the Sun, while in June the Northern Hemisphere receives the most sunlight. This gives us the seasons. The summer in the Northern Hemisphere is in June, July, and August, while in the Southern Hemisphere it is in December, January, and February.

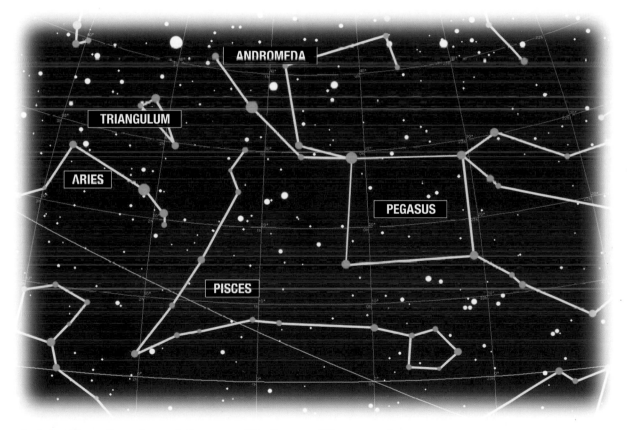

A chain of stars from the top left corner of the Square of Pegasus makes up the body of Andromeda.

THE CONSTELLATIONS

There are currently 88 constellations recognized by the International Astronomical Union. These are based on the 48 constellations listed by Greek astronomer Ptolemy in 150 CE, although he was influenced by earlier Greek, Mesopotamian, and Egyptian astronomers. But these are just the Western constellations. Cultures all over the world have created different groupings of the stars. Chinese astronomers recognize more constellations than scientists do in the West, but they are smaller.

The stars in constellations may appear next to each other like a connect-the-dots diagram and may look equally bright, but in fact they are usually at very different distances from Earth. For example, Alnitak, the star at the left of Orion's Belt, is 817 light years from Earth, while Alnilam, the star in the middle of Orion's Belt, is 1,340 light years away.

This part of the sky is visible from December to March—winter in the Northern Hemisphere, summer in the Southern Hemisphere. At the center of the map you can see Orion. If we imagined the Earth's Equator extending into the sky, Orion would be half in the Northern Hemisphere, half in the Southern Hemisphere. As this map is centered around the Equator, the stars cannot be seen in the far north or the far south. Five of the ten brightest stars in the heavens are in this part of the sky. They are: Sirius in Canis Major; Capella in Auriga; Rigel and Betelgeuse in Orion; and Procyon in Canis Minor.

Follow the downward line of Orion's Belt and you come to Sirius, the brightest star in the entire night sky.

AROUND ORION

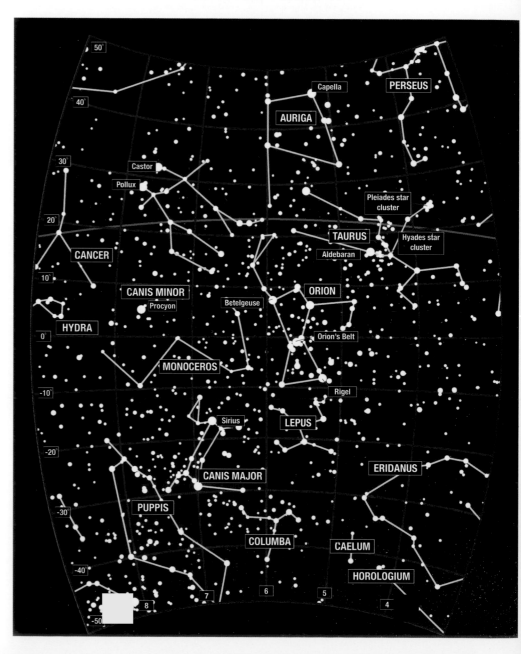

THE SKY OF LEO

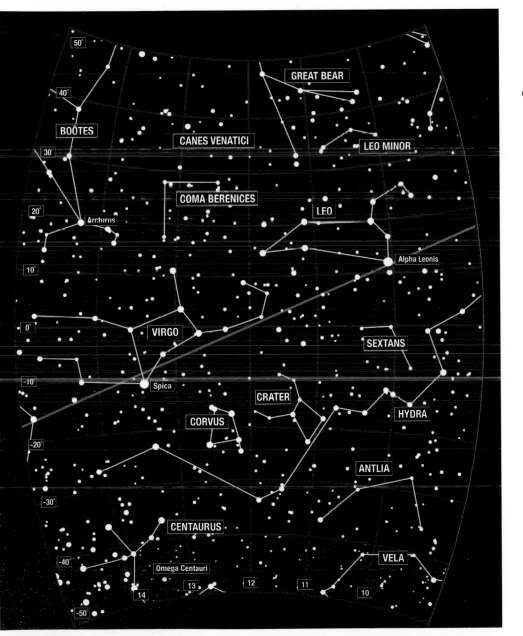

This part of the sky is visible from March until June—spring in the Northern Hemisphere, fall in the Southern Hemisphere. In the far right the sickle shape of Leo can be seen. To the south is the very long constellation of the snaky Hydra.

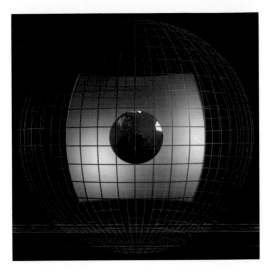

THE ZODIAC

Like the Sun, the stars appear to rise in the east and set in the west. This is because the Earth spins on its axis, passing by the stars, which are stationary. And although the sky is huge, the Sun, the Moon, and the planets actually move against a background of stars in a very narrow band of sky. The stars along this path have been divided into 12 constellations called the Zodiac, which is Greek for "circle of animals"—11 of the 12 constellations are animals (Libra, the Scales, is the 12th). The Zodiac is a way of dividing up the Sun's motion through the year.

Although we say that the stars come out at night, they are actually there during the day as well, but the glare of the Sun makes them invisible. If we could see the stars behind the Sun during the day, we would see how the sun passes through the constellations of the Zodiac.

READING STAR MAPS

When we look at a land map, we imagine that we are looking down on the Earth, but when we look at a star map, we should picture ourselves lying on our back, staring up at the stars. This makes a difference in how we read maps. On a land map, the left-hand side of the map represents west and the right-hand side east. But if you hold a star map up to the skies, the left of the map is east and the right of the map is west. Similarly, if you lie on your back during the day with your head facing north and your feet facing south, your left arm will be to your east, while your right arm is to your west. So, if a star map says "southeast of Orion," you need to look down and left, not down and right as you would on a land map.

This part of the sky is visible from June to September—summer in the Northern Hemisphere and winter in the Southern Hemisphere. It includes the brightest parts of the Milky Way. Hercules can be seen in the upper part of the map. The curl of the tail of Scorpius can be seen at the bottom of the map. Also in the lower part of the map is Sagittarius.

NORTHERN SUMMER SKIES

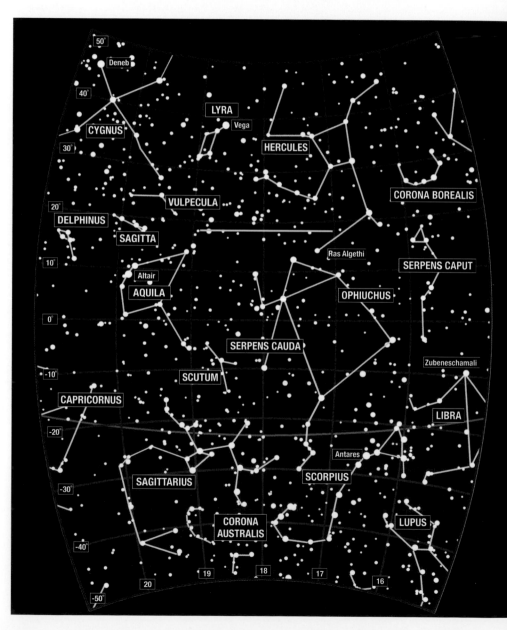

THE SKY ABOVE THE SOUTH POLE

This map covers the sky centered around the South Pole. Apart from some of the southern U.S. states, most of these constellations are not visible from the United States and Canada. The constellation Carina can be seen in the bottom left and Alpha Centauri, the third brightest star in the sky, in the bottom right.

DOS AND DON'TS

Never look directly at the Sun through binoculars or sunglasses. This can cause permanent eye damage.

If you decide to go stargazing at night, go with a parent. You will need a flashlight to help find your way and read your star maps, but take one that has a red light or with a filter to limit the amount of white light in its beam. This is because your eyes need to become used to the darkness to see the stars better.

STARGAZING

The constellations in this book were almost all named more than a thousand years ago, and their stories are often even older. We have found our way by the stars, told stories about them, and have even been comforted by them. After all, we don't know what will happen to us tomorrow, we can't be sure about the weather, but we do know what patterns the stars will make. Here are 40 of them.

Andromeda

Andromeda and her mother Cassiopeia, Queen of Ethiopia, were both beautiful, but while Andromeda was shy, her mother was vain. When Cassiopeia boasted that her daughter's beauty was greater than that of the Nereids, who were immortal sea nymphs, the sea monster Cetus was sent to ravage the land. Only sacrificing Andromeda to Cetus would stop the attacks. Cepheus, Andromeda's father, wept as he chained Andromeda to a rock and left her as a sacrifice to the sea monster. From the depths of the sea, the monster rose, saw his prey, and began to advance toward Andromeda. But all was not lost. The hero Perseus, who had just killed the Gorgon Medusa, was flying past on his winged slippers.

▶ Perseus saw something so still, beautiful, and gray that he thought it must be a statue. In fact, it was Andromeda, who was so scared that she couldn't move and whose color had drained from her cheeks. Perseus was prepared to rescue this beauty, but first he stopped to ask her parents for her hand in marriage. Andromeda was already promised to somebody else, but they reluctantly agreed that Perseus could marry her. Only when they had agreed to the marriage was Perseus prepared to risk fighting Cetus. Swooping down, he thrust his sword into Cetus and killed the beast.

Where in the sky?

Andromeda's constellation is shaped like a long "V." The easiest way to find it is to first find the Great Square of stars in Pegasus. The "V" begins at one of the corners of the Great Square. Throughout the night the constellations wheel across the sky, sometimes appearing on their sides or upside down.

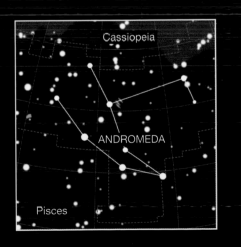

Did you know?

● It is believed that Andromeda was chained to the rocks on the coast near Joppa, an ancient city in Palestine on the eastern Mediterranean.

● Cetus is the fourth largest constellation. As it sprawls across the Equator, it is visible from most parts of the world.

● In some versions of this story, Perseus rides Pegasus, the winged horse, to Andromeda's rescue.

● What is the farthest thing that the eye can see without a telescope? It is a fuzzy mark on the hip of Andromeda, and it is about 2.7 million light years away. In fact, this mark is a huge collection of stars known as the Andromeda Galaxy, and it would take a rocket traveling at the speed of light more than two million years to get there.

Aquarius

In Greek mythology, the constellation Aquarius is known as the water-carrier and is shown as a young man carrying water in a jar. But even before the ancient Greeks, the Egyptians had connected the constellation with water. In the spring, the constellation would be seen to rise out of the River Nile, and rain showers would soon follow. These flooded the Nile, but the floods were welcomed because they fertilized the dry desert soil. In Babylonian culture, in what would be present-day Iraq, the constellation was identified with the god Ea, who was often pictured with an overflowing cup. So, Aquarius has been shown for thousands of years to be a water-carrier or even an overflowing cup, pouring water down from the heavens onto the Earth.

▶ Ganymede was the most beautiful boy alive. He was watching over his flock of sheep one day when Zeus, king of the gods, noticed him. Zeus was so struck by the boy's beauty that he decided he must bring Ganymede to live among the gods on Mount Olympus. Changing himself into an eagle, Zeus swooped down and carried off Ganymede in his eagle's talons. From then on, Ganymede worked as a water-carrier for the gods. In his constellation he is shown pouring wine. The eagle was also immortalized in the constellation Aquila, which is found next to Aquarius.

Where in the sky?

Aquarius is best seen in the evening sky in the fall in the Northern Hemisphere or in the spring in the Southern Hemisphere. From the Northern Hemisphere, it appears in the southern sky, while south of the Equator it is found overhead or high in the northern sky.

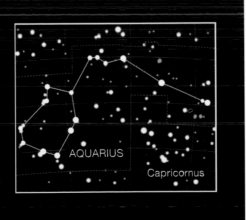

AQUARIUS

Capricornus

Did you know?

● Aquarius is found in a region of the sky that is often called the Sea because it contains constellations with watery associations, such as Cetus the sea monster, Pisces the fish, and Eridanus the river.

● In other stories, it is Deucalion, not Ganymede, who becomes the constellation Aquarius. Like the Bible story of Noah, Deucalion and his wife built a ship to survive a flood. After nine days at sea, they reached the higher land of Mount Parnassus in Greece.

● The Sun passes through the constellation of Aquarius from the third week of February to the second week of March each year.

● From ancient Greece, the story of the constellation of Aquarius passed into the Hindi Zodiac in India, where it is known as the Kumbha, which also means "water pitcher."

The constellation Aquila has been pictured as an eagle since as long ago as 1200 BCE. Birds and eagles played a major role in Greek mythology. To the ancient Greeks, all birds were ruled by Zeus and eagles would gather up his thunderbolts. Also, Aquila represented the birds that appeared to Zeus as an omen that he should go to war against the Titans. When Meropes, king of the island of Cos, was grief-stricken after his wife had died, the goddess Hera turned him into an eagle. And when Aphrodite rejected the love of Hermes, Zeus sent an eagle to snatch her sandal and carry it to Hermes. Hermes would only return the sandal if Aphrodite accepted his love.

▶ The Titan Prometheus taught humankind the arts and sciences, which Zeus felt were too great to be given to simple humans. Then when Prometheus also brought humans the gift of fire, Zeus knew that he had gone too far. He was angry with Prometheus and punished him. Prometheus was chained to a pillar in the mountains where, from dawn to dusk, Aquila the eagle would tear through his flesh and eat his liver. But because Prometheus was immortal, each night his liver would heal and the following morning Aquila would return to peck it out all over again.

Where in the sky?

Aquila is a small constellation just south of Cygnus. Lying on the Equator, it can be seen from all but the most extreme northern and southern parts of the globe. It is best seen on summer nights.

Altair

AQUILA

Did you know?

● Prometheus's agony continued until the centaur Chiron agreed to give up his immortality in exchange for Prometheus's freedom. After Prometheus had been released from being chained to the pillar, Hercules shot Aquila through the heart.

● In some versions of the myth of Ganymede, it is Aquila who carried him on Zeus's instruction to Mount Olympus.

● Many stars were named by Arab astronomers. The name of Aquila's brightest star, Altair, comes from the Arabic for " flying vulture."

● The constellations haven't always been grouped in the patterns we see today. The Greek astronomer Ptolemy in the 2nd century CE first divided the southern part of Aquila into a separate constellation called Antinous, but today this is all recognized as part of Aquila.

Aries

Aries the Ram is the first constellation in the Zodiac. In Greek mythology, the hero Jason was sent to retrieve the ram's Golden Fleece, which was guarded by the Colchis Dragon—a beast that never slept. To complete his task, Jason gathered together the heroes who made up the Argonauts and they set sail on their ship the *Argo*. After many adventures, they reached the kingdom of Colchis, where King Aeetes's daughter, Medea, fell in love with Jason. She helped him by making a magic potion that sent the dragon to sleep. Jason was then able to creep behind the dragon, steal the fleece that was hanging from an oak tree, and escape with Medea from Colchis.

▶ King Athamas's second wife, Ino, didn't like her stepchildren, Phrixus and Helle, from the king's first marriage to the cloud nymph Nephele. Plotting to have the children killed, Ino caused a famine in her husband's kingdom. Then when the king appealed to the Oracle of Delphi for advice, Ino bribed the messenger to report that Phrixus must be sacrificed to save the harvest. Devastated, Athamas was about to sacrifice his son when Nephele sent down the winged ram to save him. When Phrixus climbed onto the ram's back, Helle quickly joined him. But in the sky, Helle lost her grip, fell into the sea, and drowned.

Where in the sky?

Aries is fairly small and not distinctive. It lies to the west of Taurus and east of Pisces. It is best seen on winter nights. Its brightest star is Hamal, which means "lamb" in Arabic. Hamal marks the head of the ram.

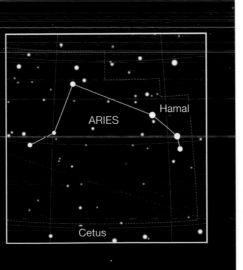

Did you know?

● The Greeks named the place where Helle fell, between the Mediterranean and the Black Seas, as the Hellespont, which means the "sea of Helle."

● In the Northern Hemisphere, Aries is associated with the fertility of spring, and, of course, lambs are born in spring. Some ancient cultures also sacrificed lambs to thank the gods for the new growth of their crops and birth of livestock in springtime. Aries used to mark the spring equinox (March 22), the day on which at noon the Sun is directly above the Equator and the days in the Northern Hemisphere are equal in length to those in the Southern Hemisphere.

● In Peru in the Southern Hemisphere, Aries appears in fall and so is connected with a harvest festival.

Auriga

Auriga is the Latin word for charioteer, and there are two stories about charioteers connected to the constellation. In one, Erichthonius, the inventor of the four-horse chariot, went into battle against Amphictyon and, on defeating him, became king of Athens. In another story, King Oenomaus couldn't bear the thought of his daughter Hippodamia marrying. To avoid having to give her away, he challenged to a chariot race any man who wanted to marry Hippodamia. If the young man won the race, he could marry Hippodamia, but if he lost he would be executed. As Oenomaus was an excellent charioteer and his horses couldn't be beaten, each young man who wanted to marry his daughter was defeated and killed.

▶ Pelops was in love with Hippodamia and plotted with Myrtilus, Oenomaus's charioteer, to win the race. They planned that Myrtilus would weaken the king's wheels by using wax rather than metal pins in the axle. In return, Pelops promised Myrtilus that he would share Oenomaus's kingdom with him if he won. But Myrtilus had a secret: He was also in love with Hippodamia. During the race, the wheels fell off Oenomaus's chariot and the king was dragged to his death. Afterward, Pelops, Hippodamia, and Myrtilus celebrated, but Hippodamia rejected Myrtilus's love. Pelops then kicked Myrtilus out of the chariot and the charioteer fell to his death.

Where in the sky?

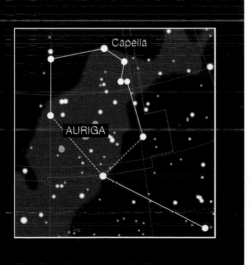

Capella

AURIGA

A striking constellation in the Northern Hemisphere's winter skies, Auriga lies to the north of the horns of Taurus. It reaches its highest point in December. It contains Capella, the sixth brightest star in the sky.

Did you know?

● From earliest times, Auriga has often been shown cradling a goat, and Capella, the name of its brightest star, means "she-goat." It is not known why the story of the charioteer and a goat are now mixed together.

● Before Pelops took his turn at racing Oenomaus, a dozen other young men had tried and failed to beat the king, and had been beheaded.

● After Myrtilus's death, his father, the messenger god Hermes, placed him among the constellations.

● The southern peninsula of Greece, the Peloponnese, was named after Pelops.

● Not a chariot but similar, in Chinese astronomy a constellation using most of the same stars as Auriga is called "Five Carriages."

Boötes

Boötes—pronounced Boh-oh-tease—is a herdsman or a hunter and is thought to represent different characters in Greek mythology. In some stories, he was the son of Demeter, goddess of the harvest. Another myth says that he was given a place among the constellations because he had invented the plow—his constellation is near the Plow, or Big Dipper, which is part of the constellation the Great Bear. While we know that many of the stories of the Greek constellations were influenced by earlier tales created by the Egyptians and Mesopotamians, the Native Americans had no contact with that part of the world. So it is surprising to learn that even among the Shawnee people of North America, the star Arcturus in Boötes also represents a hunter.

▶ Arcas was the son of Zeus and the nymph Callisto, but was brought up by Callisto's father, Lycaon, along with Lycaon's sons. One day Lycaon was visited by Zeus and was asked to prepare a meal for the god. Wanting to test whether his guest really was Zeus, Lycaon killed Arcas and served his chopped-up body as dinner. Zeus easily recognized the flesh of his own son and, enraged, turned Lycaon into a wolf, before striking his sons dead with a thunderbolt. Zeus then collected the parts of Arcas's body and brought him back to life. Arcas was later set in the stars as Boötes.

Where in the sky?

Boötes is a kite-shaped constellation seen in the Northern Hemisphere in spring and early summer, reaching its highest point around May 1. It lies to the northeast of Virgo. To find Arcturus, its brightest star, continue the curve of the handle of the Big Dipper.

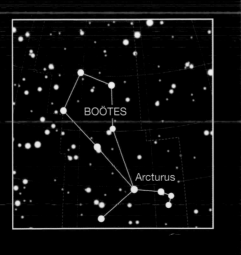

BOÖTES

Arcturus

Did you know?

● Boötes was known to the ancient Greeks as Arctophylax, which means "Bear Watcher." The bear that it is watching is the Great Bear constellation. If you look at the movement of the stars, you'll see Boötes following the Great Bear across the night sky.

● Boötes's star Arcturus, which means "bear guard," is the fourth brightest star in our galaxy. It is a red giant about 24 times larger than the Sun. It is 36 light years away from the Earth.

● In early January, the Quadrantid meteor shower comes from Boötes. Meteor showers happen as the Earth crosses the path of a disintegrated comet and moves through its debris.

● In Hawaii, Boötes marked the path for the mythical hero Hawaiiloa on his return to Hawaii from the South Pacific Ocean.

Cancer

Sometimes the stars within the constellations have their own stories. In Cancer we find the stars Asellus Borealis and Asellus Australis, which are Latin names for "the northern donkey" and "the southern donkey." According to one myth, the gods once rode on the backs of donkeys when approaching a battle against the Giants. Having never heard the braying of donkeys before, the Giants imagined an immense monster heading for them and they fled. After that, the god Dionysus put the donkeys in the sky. To the ancient Egyptians, the constellation Cancer was Khephri, the god of the summer rising sun, which was represented by the scarab beetle. To the Greeks, Cancer was also a small creature—a crab.

► Having offended the goddess Hera, the hero Hercules was set Twelve Labors to complete. The second of these was to kill the Hydra of Lerna, a multi-headed serpent that Hera had raised to defeat him. With his club, a sword, and a sickle, Hercules attacked the Hydra, but each time he cut off one of its heads, another two grew from the stump. While Hercules was fighting, a crab crept out of the swamp and bit him on the foot before Hercules was able to crush it. Hera then placed the crab among the constellations.

Where in the sky?

Cancer is the hardest constellation of the Zodiac to see. It is small, not very bright, and is found between Gemini and Leo. It is at its highest point at the end of January or the beginning of February.

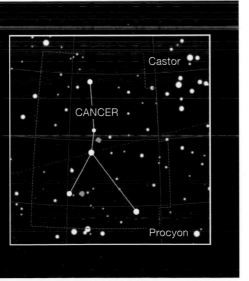

Did you know?

● Looking through telescopes, astronomers can see a huge cloud of dust in Cancer. This is the Crab Nebula and is what is left of a star after it exploded. The star was a supernova that was so bright that it could be seen during the day. Chinese astronomers observed the creation of this supernova almost 1,000 years ago.

● The stars of Cancer once marked the position of the Sun on June 21, the longest day of the year in the Northern Hemisphere. To the Mesopotamians, souls were thought to pass to the Underworld on the longest day of the year. In Egypt, the scarab beetle—which they associated with the constellation—would have appeared after the Nile summer floods each year, exactly when the Sun was in Cancer.

● When a star appears to twinkle, it is not the star that is changing, but the hot and cold air in the Earth's atmosphere bending the path of the light coming from the star.

Canis Major

Canis Major means "the Greater Dog." The constellation has been associated with different dogs in mythology, including a dog that failed to protect Princess Europa from Zeus when he appeared to her as a bull, as well as one of Orion the Hunter's dogs, and also the multi-headed dog Cerberus. The constellation includes Sirius, the brightest star in the sky, which is also known as the Dog Star. Ancient Egyptians based their calendar on Sirius: After being absent from the skies for 70 days, Sirius would reappear just before sunrise. As this happened in the summer months before the summer solstice—when the Sun is at its highest in the Northern Hemisphere—Sirius became associated with the hottest time of the year.

The final of Hercules's Twelve Labors was to bring the dog Cerberus back to King Eurystheus. Cerberus guarded the gates of the Underworld, allowing people to enter, but preventing anyone from leaving. Not only did Hercules have to risk entering the Underworld, but under the conditions set by Eurystheus he wasn't allowed to use any weapons against Cerberus. Hercules, however, was so strong that he managed to overpower Cerberus with his bare hands. Having succeeded, Hercules dragged Cerberus's body back to Eurystheus. When the king saw the monstrous dog, he was so scared that he leapt into a giant jar.

Where in the sky?

Canis Major can be found from the constellation Orion. Find the three stars in Orion's Belt and extend the line that they form to the southeast. This will lead directly to Sirius, the star that marks the jaw of Canis Major.

Did you know?

● Cerberus was the offspring of the giant monster Typhon and Echidna, who had the head of a woman and the body of a serpent. Cerberus's siblings were the dragon Ladon and the Hydra.

● At one time in ancient Egypt, Sirius was identified with the jackal-headed Egyptian god Anubis, who guided the dead to the Underworld.

● The name Sirius comes from the Greek for "scorching." From Sirius the Dog Star we have the term "Dog Days," meaning the hottest part of the year.

● Sirius is actually two stars orbiting each other. It is so bright partly because it is only nine light years away—there aren't many stars closer to Earth than that. It is also gradually moving closer to the Solar System.

Canis Minor

Canis Minor means "the lesser dog." In one Arabic story, Canis Major and Canis Minor were two sisters, but when Canis Major fell in love and left her sister, Canis Minor was alone and wept. In Greek mythology, Canis Minor has become associated with different stories. In one myth, along with Canis Major, it is one of Orion the Hunter's hounds. In another myth, it is Maera, the dog of Icarius, who was murdered by the people of Athens when they mistakenly thought that he had poisoned their shepherds. Maera led Icarius's daughter, Erigone, to the man's body. Grief-stricken, Erigone hanged herself, and Maera leapt off a cliff to its death. To atone for their mistake, the Athenians established a yearly festival celebrating Icarius and Erigone.

▶ In another story, the Teumessian fox was a giant among foxes and had been sent to attack the children of Thebes. Seeking help, the people of Thebes found Laelaps, a magical dog that could catch anything it chased. But the Teumessian fox could never be caught. Laelaps would chase and could even snap at the fox's heels, but he could never catch the fox. Their story is played out in the stars, with Canis Minor as the Teumessian fox, rising before Canis Major as Laelaps. They move through the night sky together, but Canis Major never catches up with Canis Minor.

Where in the sky?

Canis Minor is a small constellation, but its main star, Procyon, is the eighth brightest star in the sky. Canis Minor lies due south of the Gemini twins on the other side of the Milky Way from Canis Major.

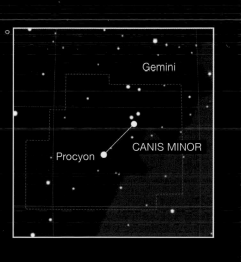

Gemini

Procyon

CANIS MINOR

Did you know?

● It was said that because the chase between Laelaps and the Teumessian fox could never be completed, Zeus turned the two animals into stone and placed them in the heavens.

● Canis Minor is most clearly visible in the evening sky from January to March.

● Some say that Maera threw itself down a well rather than over a cliff and became Canis Major, not Canis Minor.

● Canis Minor only used to include its brightest star, Procyon, which means "before the dog." It is "before the dog" because the star rises before Sirius, the Dog Star.

Capricornus

Was it a crocodile? An antelope? A hippopotamus? Capricornus has been all these, but to the Babylonians in 1000 BCE and to the ancient Greeks who came later, it was a sea-goat. But it didn't begin in the sea. In life, Capricornus, whose name means "horned goat," was Pan, a goat or perhaps a satyr—a man with goats' legs—who was the god of the fields, the forests, and music. He invented the musical panpipes. Pan also enjoyed frightening herds of animals by surprising them with his shrill shriek and, at times, causing them to stampede. From this feeling of sudden, uncontrollable fear we have the word "panic." Pan was a trickster, but was forgiven when he put his shriek to good use.

► In the great battle between the Titans and the Olympian Gods, the giant Typhon was sent to destroy the Olympians. As the monster approached, Pan dived into the River Nile and tried to turn himself into a fish to escape. But he only managed to transform half his body: he grew a fish's tail, but kept his goat's head. Typhon reached Zeus, managing to pull out his sinews, before Pan let out a shriek so piercing that even Typhon was frightened for a moment. Seizing the opportunity, the other Olympian gods were able to disguise themselves as animals and make their escape.

Where in the sky?

Capricornus is at its highest at midnight in August, but light summer skies and its location south of the Equator make it hard to see in the more northerly parts of the Northern Hemisphere. It sits between Sagittarius and Aquarius.

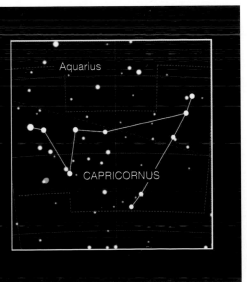

Aquarius

CAPRICORNUS

Did you know?

● After escaping Typhon, Pan and Hermes gathered together Zeus's body parts. Once his strength had been restored, Zeus pursued Typhon. He finally cut down the monster with thunderbolts and buried him under the volcano in Mount Etna, on the island of Sicily.

● When the Tropic of Capricorn was named 2,000 years ago, the Sun was in the direction of Capricornus on December 21. Due to a wobble in the Earth's axis, these days the Sun is in the direction of Sagittarius on December 21.

● The winter solstice (December 21) is the shortest day of the year in the Northern Hemisphere and the longest day of the year in the Southern Hemisphere. On December 21, the Sun at noon is directly above the Tropic of Capricorn.

● Capricornus is the smallest constellation in the Zodiac.

Carina

Carina is part of what was once a larger constellation of Argo Navis—the ship. In 1763, the astronomer Nicolas Louis de Lacaille divided Argo Navis into three smaller parts: Carina, meaning the keel of a ship; Puppis, a ship's raised poop deck; and Vela, the ship's sails. To the Babylonians, *Argo Navis* had been the ship that a mortal had built, like Noah's Ark, to escape a flood. To the ancient Greeks it was the *Argo*, the ship of Jason and the Argonauts. Jason was set the task of recovering the Golden Fleece of a ram from a grove where it was guarded by the Colchis Dragon. With a crew of Greek heroes, he set sail.

▶ On the *Argo's* journey, Jason had to navigate between the clashing rocks of the Symplegades, which crushed anything that tried to pass between them. Phineas, an old man who could see into the future, told them to release a dove shortly before the *Argo* reached the Symplegades. As they approached the rocks, they released the dove and it flew between the rocks, causing them to clash. While the rocks were parting again, the Argonauts rowed as fiercely as they could. The rocks began to close in, but the *Argo* made it through just before they clashed again.

Where in the sky?

Carina lies partly in the Milky Way and can't be seen at more northern latitudes. It is at its highest at midnight in the southern summer months. It includes Canopus, the second brightest star in the night sky.

Canopus

CARINA

Did you know?

● Jason has to sail from the Mediterranean Sea to the Black Sea, so it's likely that the clashing rocks of the Symplegades refer to the narrower waters at the Bosporus, where the two seas meet.

● After the *Argo* had made it through the Symplegades, the rocks never clashed again.

● The dove released from the *Argo* can be seen in the constellation Columba.

● The star Canopus represents one of the steering oars at the stern of the *Argo*.

● Carina includes a unique star, Eta Carinae, which flared up in 1843 to become even brighter than Canopus. It is now no longer visible to the naked eye. Astronomers think that Eta Carinae is a young star that will one day explode.

Cassiopeia

With its "W" shape, Cassiopeia is one of the most easily recognized northern constellations. Near the North Star, she can be used to find the general direction of the North Pole. Also, Cassiopeia and her husband Cepheus, King of Ethiopia, are the only husband and wife among the constellations and are placed in the heavens next to each other. As a queen in life, Cassiopeia would have had a throne, but as a constellation she appears, at times, hanging upside down and is sometimes seen tied to a chair. Why is she being punished like this? The clue is that she is playing with her hair—in her story, her vanity and arrogance almost destroyed her family as well as her kingdom.

► While combing her hair one day, Cassiopeia boasted to the 50 Nereids, who were beautiful, immortal sea nymphs, that she and her daughter, Andromeda, were more beautiful than they were. Angered by Cassiopeia's arrogance, the Nereids looked to Poseidon, the god of the sea, to punish the mortal. Poseidon struck his trident into the water, causing a flood. Then he summoned up a sea monster, Cetus, to ravage the coastline. An oracle told Cepheus the only thing that would stop Cetus's attacks was to sacrifice his daughter Andromeda to the sea monster. Or would Andromeda be rescued? See the entry for Andromeda's constellation to find out what happened.

Where in the sky?

Cassiopeia sits on the opposite side of the North Star from the Big Dipper. Immediately to her east is her husband Cepheus. To the south of Cassiopeia is her daughter Andromeda. Even farther south is the constellation of Cetus.

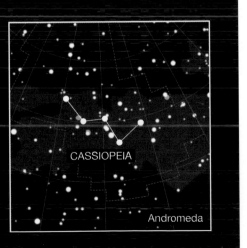

CASSIOPEIA

Andromeda

Did you know?

● In punishment for her vanity, Cassiopeia was placed in the heavens by Poseidon as a constellation that would sometimes appear upside down.

● The constellation of Cepheus, Cassiopeia's husband, is easy to find because it is near the North Star and its five stars form the shape of a house with a steep roof.

● Andromeda was rescued from Cetus by Perseus, who wanted to marry her. As she had already been promised to a man called Phineus, a fight broke out. Perseus ended the dispute by pulling out the Gorgon Medusa's head from his bag. This turned Phineus to stone, leaving Perseus free to marry Andromeda.

Centaurus

Centaurs—who had the head and torso of a man, but the body and legs of a horse—were wild and savage, particularly after drinking wine. But there were two civilized centaurs. One was their leader, Chiron, who was immortal, kind, and wise—he even taught humans hunting and music. He had been educated by the gods and had himself been Hercules's tutor. The other civilized centaur was Pholus. While Hercules was on his way to complete his Third Labor and capture the Erymanthian Boar, he was offered dinner by Pholus. But when the other centaurs saw Hercules dining with a centaur and drinking their wine, they became upset and began throwing rocks at the hero.

▶ Hercules responded to the centaurs' attack by firing arrows—arrows that he had dipped in the Hydra's blood. Chiron wasn't involved in the fight, but one of Hercules's arrows accidentally hit him. The Hydra's blood poisoned Chiron and he was unable to heal himself. But as he was immortal, nor could he die. Instead, he would remain in agony forever. Around the same time, Prometheus, also an immortal, was cursed to have his liver pecked out every day by the eagle Aquila. The curse could only be lifted by another immortal sacrificing itself. Chiron agreed to sacrifice himself to help Prometheus, ending both their agonies.

Where in the sky?

Centaurus is high in the sky during the southern fall months. It contains Alpha Centauri, the third brightest star in the sky and the star that is closest to the Sun. Alpha Centauri marks the left front leg of the centaur.

CENTAURUS

Omega Centauri

Alpha Centauri

Did you know?

● Centaurus contains Omega Centauri, the largest and brightest globular star cluster visible from Earth.

● The origins of Centaurus can be found as early as Babylonian culture, where the constellation was recognized as a "bison-man"—a bison with a human head.

● It is possible that the myth of centaurs was created when people who had never seen horses before first witnessed someone riding on horseback—at first glance, horse and man might have seemed to be one animal. It was reported that when the Aztecs of Mexico—who had never seen horses before—first saw Spanish invaders on horseback, they imagined that the horse and man were a single monster that could separate into either a man or a horse when it chose to.

Corona Borealis

Corona Borealis means "the Northern Crown." It is the crown of Ariadne, daughter of King Minos of Crete. Every nine years, seven young men and seven young women were sent by King Aegeus of Athens to the island of Crete as tribute to King Minos. Once on Crete they would be thrown into a maze known as the Labyrinth. Inside the Labyrinth lived the Minotaur—a fierce creature that had the head of a bull and the body of a man. No one had ever been able to find his way out of the Labyrinth, nor survive an encounter with the Minotaur. But Theseus, King Aegeus's son, volunteered to be one of the young Athenians sent to Crete. He was going to try to defeat the Minotaur.

▶ On Crete, Ariadne fell in love with Theseus. To help him kill the Minotaur, she gave him a golden ball of twine. With this, he could leave a trail of his path through the Labyrinth and would be able to find his way out again. As he made his way through the corridors, Theseus unwound the twine until he came face to face with the Minotaur. When the beast charged at him, Theseus drew his sword and killed it. Then, using the twine, he followed the trail back out of the Labyrinth. With Ariadne and the other young Athenians, Theseus escaped from Crete.

Where in the sky?

Corona Borealis is a small constellation that lies between Boötes to the west and Hercules to the east. It reaches its highest point at midnight in mid-May. As the circle of stars is incomplete, early Arab astronomers called the constellation "the Broken Platter."

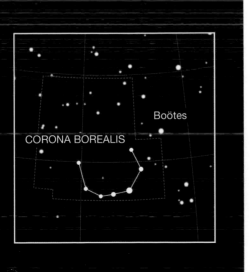

Boötes

CORONA BOREALIS

Did you know?

● Theseus had promised his father that if he died in Crete, his ship would return with black sails, but if he survived, the ship would sail with white sails. In the excitement of Theseus's victory, he forgot to change the sails from black to white. When his father saw the black sails approaching, he threw himself off a cliff and died.

● Theseus later left Ariadne on the island of Naxos. In one version of the story, Ariadne married the god Dionysus and the Corona Borealis represents the crown she wore at her wedding. In another version, after Theseus left Ariadne, she died of a broken heart.

● There is a constellation in the Southern Hemisphere called Corona Australis, which means "the Southern Crown."

● Although the ruins of King Minos's palace at Knossos on Crete have been found, the location of the labyrinth—if it existed—has not.

Corvus

orvus means "the crow," a bird sacred to the Greek sun-god Apollo. According to one myth, crows were once white, but when a crow flew to tell Apollo that his beloved Coronis was in love with somebody else, Apollo cursed the crow for not stopping her. The curse was so strong that it scorched the bird's feathers, turning them black forever. Still angry, Apollo then shot an arrow at Coronis, killing her. On another occasion, when the Olympian gods turned themselves into animals to escape the monster Typhon, Apollo transformed himself into a crow. In Babylonian mythology, Corvus was sacred to Adad, the god of rain—at that time the constellation would have risen just before the fall rains began.

▶ The god Apollo was about to make a sacrifice to his father, Zeus, and sent a crow to fetch water from a spring. Flying off with a bowl, the crow passed a fig tree laden with unripe fruit. Distracted from its task, the crow stopped at the tree and waited several days for the fruit to ripen. Once it had eaten the fruit, the crow picked up a water snake and flew back to Apollo, telling him that the water snake had been blocking the spring. But Apollo saw through the lie and condemned the crow to a life of thirst.

Where in the sky?

The constellations of Corvus (the crow), Crater (the bowl), and Hydra (the water snake) are next to each other in the Southern Hemisphere. Corvus is made up of four main stars that form an uneven box shape. It is a small, springtime constellation, near Virgo.

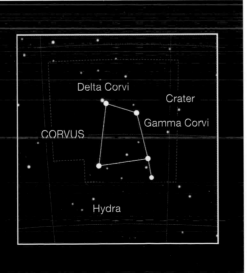

Did you know?

● In both Greek and Babylonian constellations, Corvus is shown sitting on the tail of the Hydra.

● Corvus includes a double star, Delta Corvi, at the end of its left wing. The primary star of Delta Corvi is blue-white, while the secondary star is purple-tinged.

● The brightest star in Corvus is Gamma Corvi, the star at the bird's foot.

● Drawing a line from Gamma Corvi through Delta Corvi points you toward Spica, the brightest star in Virgo and the 15th brightest star in the night sky.

● The center of Corvus contains a planetary nebula, which is an expanding shell of gas ejected from old red giant stars.

Crater

Crater the Cup is the cup of Apollo and the cup that Corvus carries when he is sent to fetch water for the god. But this is only one story. Although the stars appear in the same patterns all over the world, different cultures build different stories around them. In ancient Chinese astronomy, the Crater was identified as Yi, a mythical archer. It was believed that thousands of years ago there were ten three-legged sun-birds. Each day one of them would travel around the world in a carriage driven by the Mother of the Suns. In this way, sunlight rose in the east in the morning, crossed the sky, and set in the west in the evening.

▶ The sun-birds grew tired of their routine and decided that the ten of them would all rise at the same time. But with ten suns in the sky, the Earth became unbearably hot, crops shriveled, and lakes dried up. Dijun, God of the Eastern Heaven, sent for the archer Yi to discipline the sun-birds. But when Yi saw what the sun-birds had done, he was so angry that he shot nine of them and was about to shoot the tenth. Realizing that if Yi shot the tenth sun-bird the world would be plunged into everlasting darkness, Emperor Yao hurried to Yi and managed to stop him just in time.

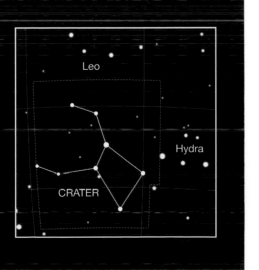

Where in the sky?

Crater is positioned just to the east of Corvus and, like Corvus, is seen balancing on the Hydra. Crater is a faint constellation, best seen in April. It reaches its highest point at midnight around March 12.

Leo

Hydra

CRATER

Did you know?

● Crater is Latin for cup.

● For saving humanity, Yi was given an elixir of immortality. Later, an apprentice of his broke into his house and tried to steal the elixir, but Yi's wife, Chang'e, wouldn't let him. To keep the elixir from the apprentice, Chang'e swallowed it. With this, she gained immortality and flew into the sky. But wanting to be near her husband, she chose to live on the Moon. She is celebrated in China and Vietnam in the Mid-Fall Festival, which is held during a full moon.

● The same side of the Moon always faces the Earth. This is because the effects of the Earth's gravitational pull on the Moon have slowed the Moon's rotation, so that it rotates only once each orbit of the Earth.

Cygnus

Cygnus is shown on star maps as a swan flying along the Milky Way. It is one of the easier constellations to spot because it is bright and its stars form a cross: the swan's tail is the top of the cross, the wings are the horizontal beam of the cross, and the swan's long neck is the cross's staff. The Northern Cross is another name for the constellation. Before the Greeks, the stars of Cygnus were identified with another bird, the mythical Roc of Mesopotamian mythology. This huge bird is featured in stories of Sinbad. When the Roc landed, Sinbad clung to its claws and was carried off to the Valley of Diamonds, where he gathered up treasure. He later returned to Baghdad a rich man.

▶ There are many Greek myths about young men being turned into swans. For example, one of the god Poseidon's sons was defeated in battle by Achilles, but Poseidon quickly turned his son into a swan and he flew away. The best-known swan story, however, is about Zeus and Leda. Zeus disguised himself as a swan and then pretended to be escaping an eagle. Leda accepted the swan into her arms, protecting it. But then Zeus changed himself back into a god and Leda fell in love with him. From their relationship were born Helen of Troy and the Gemini twins, Castor and Polydeuces.

Where in the sky?

Cygnus is easy to see in the Northern Hemisphere in the summer months. It is at its highest in July. It borders Draco and Pegasus. Its brightest star is Deneb, which marks its tail. Deneb also means "tail" in Arabic.

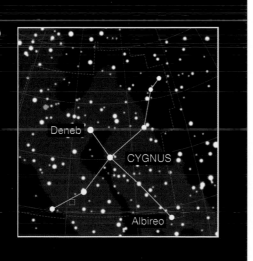

Deneb

CYGNUS

Albireo

Did you know?

● Marking the swan's beak in the constellation is Albireo, a double star colored both green and amber.

● In another version of the story, Zeus pursued the nymph Nemesis. To escape him, she turned herself into different animals. When she turned herself into a goose, he turned himself into a swan. Not recognizing that it was Zeus in disguise, Nemesis trusted the swan, but he tricked her, just as he had done Leda.

● Orbiting a huge star in the constellation Cygnus is a black hole, which is a star that is so big and has such a strong gravitational pull that nothing can escape it, not even light. Black holes are invisible, but astronomers know that the black hole in Cygnus exists because it gives off X-ray radiation.

Delphinus

We know that dolphins are friendly and intelligent, so perhaps it is not surprising that in Greek mythology there are two stories about dolphins helping humans and being rewarded with a place among the constellations. In the first story, Poseidon, god of the sea, built himself a splendid underwater palace, but soon realized that he was lonely there without a wife. He fell in love with the sea nymph Amphitrite, one of the Nereids, but at first she rejected his marriage proposal and hid among the other Nereids. When Poseidon sent a messenger with a dolphin to try to persuade her to change her mind, she returned to Poseidon and happily married him. In thanks, Poseidon placed the image of the dolphin among the stars.

▶ The other story about a dolphin tells of Arion, whose success as a musician made him wealthy. While he was traveling back from Sicily to Greece, the sailors on his ship plotted to kill him and steal his money. When the sailors surrounded him and drew their swords, Arion pleaded to be allowed to sing one last song. Playing his lyre and singing, his sweet music attracted a school of dolphins, who gathered around the ship. As the song drew to a close and the sailors prepared to kill Arion, he jumped overboard. One of the dolphins then carried Arion safely to land.

Where in the sky?

As it is situated just above the Equator, Delphinus can be seen from all around the world, except from the Antarctic. It is near the Milky Way, not far from Pegasus. It is best seen in late summer.

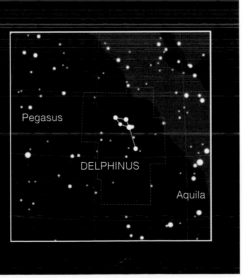

Did you know?

● When Arion reached land he told his story to Periander, the tyrant of Corinth. Not long after, the sailors arrived in Corinth and when Periander asked them about Arion, they said that he had died at sea. Periander then presented Arion in front of them and sentenced the sailors to be crucified.

● How are stars named? Many have Arabic names given to them by astronomers who were translating the ancient Greek names or who were creating new names. But two stars of Delphinus have the names "Sualocin" and "Rotanev." These are actually the words "Nicolaus" and "Venator" backward and are the Latin versions of the name Niccolo Cacciatore, a 19th-century Italian astronomer. He named the stars after himself and is the only astronomer who has managed to do so.

● Delphinus is Latin for dolphin.

Draco

A dragon, a snake, a hippopotamus, and a crocodile—the constellation Draco has been regarded as all these animals over thousands of years. But to the ancient Greeks, Draco was Ladon, the dragon offspring of the giant Typhon and Echidna, a creature that was half-woman and half-serpent. Not only was Ladon fierce, it also never slept, which made it an ideal guardian of treasure. The story goes that the goddess Hera had been given a golden apple tree as a wedding gift. At first she asked the Hesperides nymphs to guard the tree, but they kept picking the apples for themselves, so Hera brought Ladon into the garden to protect her precious fruit.

▶ Driven insane by Hera, the hero Hercules killed his children. As punishment for this, he had to complete Twelve Labors, one of which was to fetch the Hesperides' apples guarded by Ladon. Before he approached the dragon, Hercules dipped his arrows in the gall of the Hydra, poisoning them. When he shot his arrows at Ladon, the poison killed the dragon. Having been warned not to pluck the apples himself, Hercules sought the help of the Titan Atlas to reach for three apples. With his labor completed, Hercules left, and Hera placed the image of Draco in the sky.

Where in the sky?

Draco is the eighth largest constellation, but is not easily visible. It coils around the far north in the sky. Its brightest star is Eltanin, beside its right eye, which comes from the Arabic for "the serpent." One of Hercules's feet is resting on Draco's head.

North Star

DRACO

Eltanin

Boötes

Did you know?

● The day after Hercules killed Ladon, its tail still twitched and the poison in its wounds was still fresh enough to kill flies trying to feed on the body.

● In another story, the goddess Athena caught Draco by the tail and swung it into the sky. Its body became knotted around the North Pole of the stars.

● In the Mesopotamian culture before the ancient Greeks, Draco was shown as a winged dragon, but in the 6th century BCE, Greek philosopher Thales redrew the constellation without wings. With the stars that had made up Draco's wings, Thales created the constellation Little Bear (Ursa Minor). Ever since then, Draco has been wingless.

● Some versions of the story say that Ladon had 100 heads.

Equuleus

Some constellations were recognized as long ago as 5000 BCE and have different stories told about them in Mesopotamian, ancient Egyptian, and ancient Greek culture. Others, though, are only 2,000 years old. Equuleus, the second smallest constellation, was first mentioned in 150 CE in the *Almagest*, a book of astronomy written by Greek astronomer Ptolemy. Equuleus is the foal, or little horse, and might have been the horse of one of the Gemini twins, both of whom were known as good huntsmen on horseback. Another story links Equuleus with Hippe, the daughter of the centaur Chiron. Hippe was so ashamed of her love affair with a human that the gods turned her into a horse.

▶ Why is the capital city of Greece called Athens? According to Greek myth, the god Poseidon and the goddess Athena competed over who would be the patron of the city. To win the citizens' approval, each gave the city a gift. Athena offered an olive tree, the fruit of which could be eaten or turned into olive oil, while the wood and pits could be burnt and used for fuel. Poseidon struck the ground with his trident and the horse Equuleus sprang out. But the people of the city chose Athena's gift, making her the patron and naming the city after her.

Where in the sky?

Equuleus is visible in both hemispheres everywhere except from the Antarctic. It has an uneven square shape and is found southeast of Delphinus and next to the other horse, Pegasus. It reaches its highest point in early August.

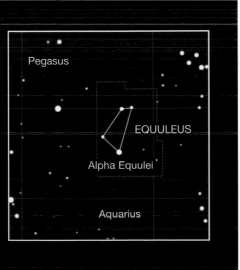

Pegasus

EQUULEUS

Alpha Equulei

Aquarius

Did you know?

● In another version of the contest to become patron of Athens, Poseidon and Athena had a race and Athena just managed to win. She planted an olive tree, while Poseidon, arriving moments later, struck the Acropolis—the city's fortress—with his trident and created the sea.

● Equuleus contains a binary star—two stars orbiting each other—in Alpha Equulei, which is the star at the base of the horse's mane.

● Like most people of his time, Ptolemy, who first recognized Equuleus, believed that the Sun and the planets orbited the Earth. Although Aristarchus in 330 BCE had suggested that the Earth and planets revolved around the Sun, rather than the Sun around the Earth, his view was not accepted until 1543, when astronomer Nicolaus Copernicus proved that the Sun is the center of the Solar System.

Eridanus

The sixth largest constellation, Eridanus the River, is like many rivers, long and winding. Its story is also one of a winding, tragic journey. Opinions differ over whether it represents the River Nile in Egypt, the River Euphrates in Iraq, or the River Po in Italy. But in each case the story remains the same: Phaethon was a mortal but he was the son of the sun-god Helios and the sea-nymph Clymene. Not having been brought up by his father, when Phaethon was old enough, he went to Helios's palace to find him. To prove to Phaethon that he was his father, Helios said that he would grant the boy any wish—a promise that he would come to regret.

▶ Phaethon asked his father to be allowed to drive the chariot that carries the Sun, rising in the morning, flying across the sky, and setting in the evening. Reluctantly, Helios agreed, but the inexperienced Phaethon soon lost control of the chariot. The horses pulling the chariot veered off their path; they brushed over the tops of mountains, causing fires, burning the land, and drying up rivers. To save the world from destruction, Zeus sent a thunderbolt at the chariot, driving it to the ground and throwing Phaethon into a river. This extinguished the flames, but Phaethon was killed by the fall.

Where in the sky?

Eridanus winds from near the star Rigel at the foot of Orion into the Southern Hemisphere. It is quite faint, even in the tropics. However, at its base it does contain Achernar, the ninth brightest star in the sky.

ERIDANUS

Achernar

Did you know?

● In their grief, Phaethon's sisters, the Heliades, were transformed into poplar trees and their tears became the trees' amber-colored sap.

● Some people said that the Sahara Desert was created when Phaethon lost control of the sun-chariot and scorched the land.

● Eridanus's brightest star, Achernar, is the Arabic word for "end of the river." It is a peculiar star because it is one of the flattest stars known. Its radius is about 50 percent larger at its equator than at the poles. This distortion occurs because the star is spinning extremely rapidly.

● Eridanus contains the Eridanus Supervoid, which is an area of the Universe without any galaxies. With a diameter of about one billion light years, it is much larger than any other known void.

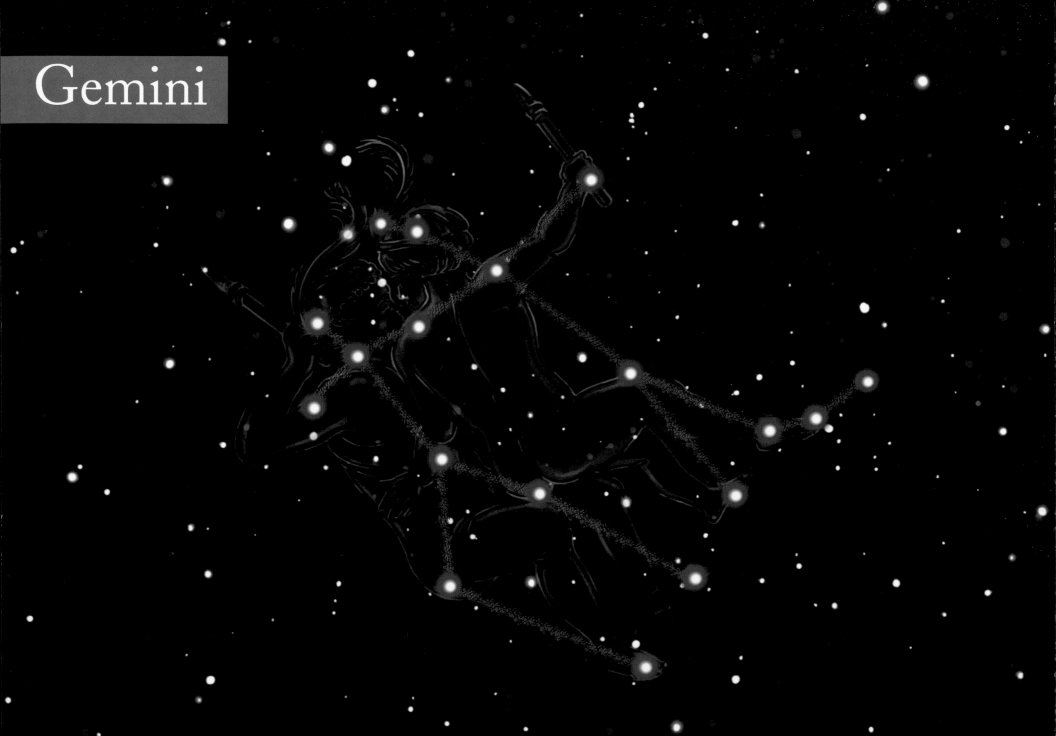

Gemini

Gemini is the Twins, and for thousands of years the two brightest stars of this constellation, Castor and Pollux, have been thought to represent twins. In ancient Egyptian mythology, the two stars were compared to a pair of sprouting plants, while in Phoenician culture, in what today is Lebanon, they were seen as a pair of kid goats. To the Greeks, they were Castor and Polydeuces, while in later Roman legends they were Romulus and Remus, the twin boys who founded the city of Rome. With a little imagination, the long lines of Gemini look a little bit like two figures next to each other. The feet of the twins paddle in the Milky Way.

▶ Although they were twins, Castor was mortal, while Polydeuces was immortal. They joined the Argonauts but on their journey clashed with two other Argonaut twins, Idas and Lynceus, over two beautiful women. Castor and Polydeuces carried the women off, but they were pursued. When Lynceus stabbed Castor, Polydeuces attacked and killed him. Zeus, meanwhile, stepped in and killed Idas with a thunderbolt. The immortal Polydeuces survived, but his twin Castor died. Not wanting to live without his brother, Polydeuces begged Zeus to remove his immortality. Zeus granted his wish and placed the twins in the stars.

Where in the sky?

Gemini is best seen in the northern winter sky, when it lies to the northeast of Orion. Part of the Zodiac, it has Cancer on one side and Taurus on the other. In December in Gemini, the Geminid meteor showers can be seen.

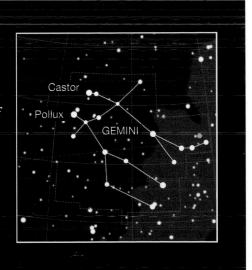

Castor
Pollux
GEMINI

Did you know?

● Castor and Polydeuces are the patron saints of sailors. During storms, sailors sometimes see an electrical glow around a ship's rigging. This is called St. Elmo's Fire. When there are two glowing parts in the rigging, they are called Castor and Polydeuces and are believed to be a good omen.

● Castor and Polydeuces aren't the only twins in Gemini. What appears to be the star Castor is actually made up of three pairs of stars, with each pair in orbit.

● On their voyage, Polydeuces boxed Amycus, the giant son of Poseidon and the world's biggest bully. When Amycus insisted someone fight him, Polydeuces offered and, even though Amycus had invented boxing and was immensely strong, Polydeuces was faster. He beat the bully.

Great Bear

Perhaps the first shape that you'll learn to recognize in the night sky is the Big Dipper, or Plow. These seven stars, which grouped together look like a pot with a long handle, are part of the constellation of the Great Bear (Ursa Major), the third largest constellation. To the Inuits, the Big Dipper is a caribou, while to the Iroquois of North America the three stars of the Great Bear's tail were three hunters chasing the bear. If you count five stars across from the tip of the tail of the bear, you have found the star Dubhe. Beneath that, at a slight angle, is Merak. If you extend a line from Merak to Dubhe and onward, you are pointing toward the North Star.

► The nymph Callisto was out hunting when Zeus fell in love with her. After she gave birth to Zeus's child, his wife, Hera, became jealous and changed Callisto into a bear. For 15 years, Callisto roamed the woods trapped in the body of a bear. Meanwhile, her son, Arcas, grew up and became a hunter. One day, Arcas was hunting when he spotted a bear—Callisto. She recognized her son, but he didn't recognize his mother. He was about to throw his spear at the bear when Zeus stopped him. Rather than allow Arcas to kill Callisto, Zeus placed the son and mother in the sky as Boötes and the Great Bear.

Where in the sky?

The seven stars of the Big Dipper make up one of the easier asterisms—patterns of stars—to find. The Big Dipper's handle begins at Alkaid and curves round. Merak marks the base of the plow farthest from Alkaid. This constellation is in the northern part of the sky and can be seen all year round.

Draco
Dubhe
Alkaid
Merak
GREAT BEAR

Did you know?

● Extend the curve of the handle away from the Big Dipper and you reach the star Arcturus in Boötes.

● Arab astronomers saw the Great Bear as a coffin and the bear's unusually long tail as a line of mourners.

● Although the constellations wheel across the sky, their shapes seem to stay the same. We can still recognize the Great Bear year after year. But actually the constellations are changing shape, albeit very slowly. The stars Alkaid and Dubhe in the Great Bear are moving through space in an opposite direction from the other stars in the constellation. In 10,000 years' time, the shape of the Great Bear will be different.

Hercules

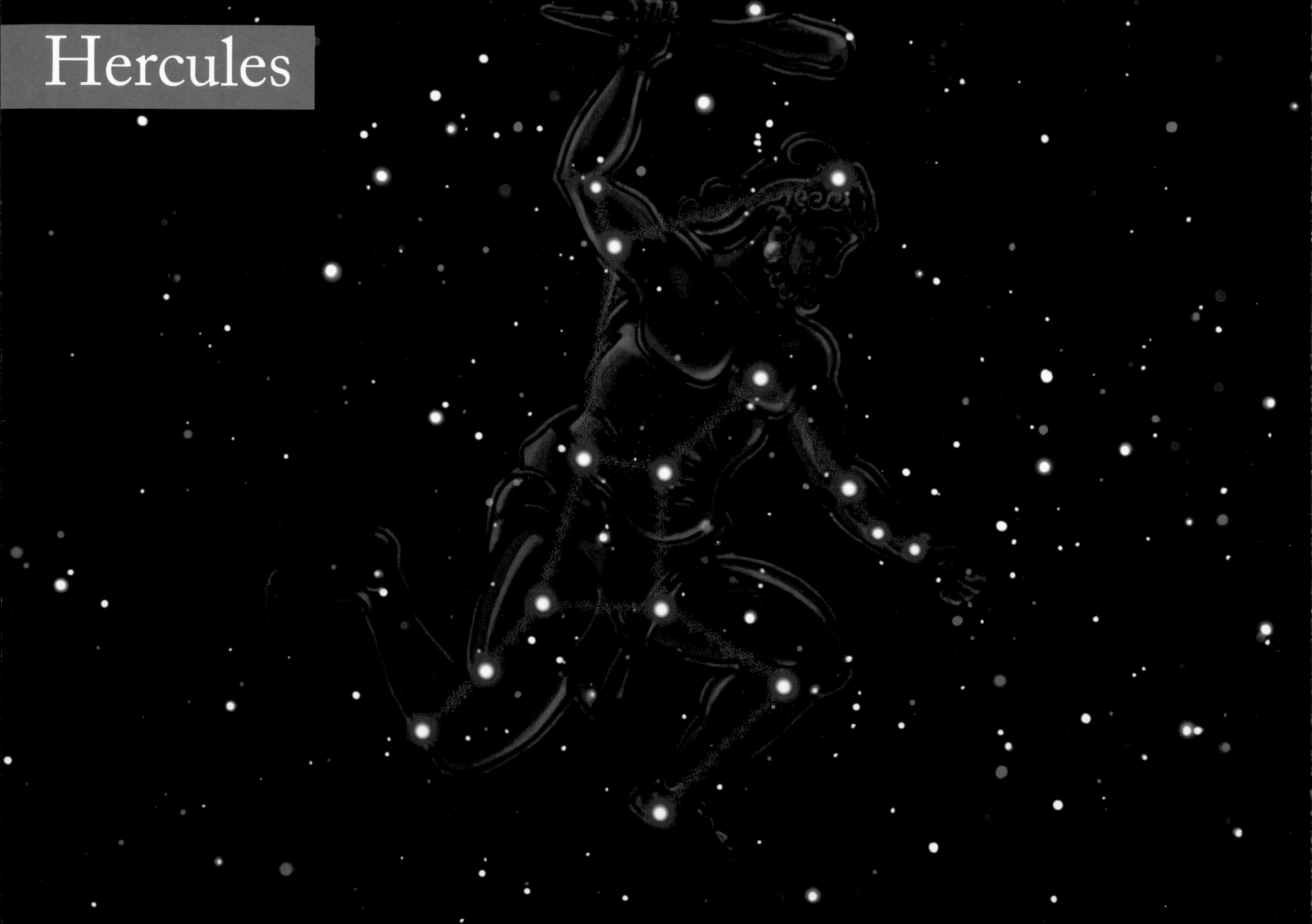

The greatest of Greek heroes, Hercules was the son of Zeus and was said to be immortal. In the end, though, he did die. But how? When Hercules's second wife Deinaeira suspected that Hercules might be falling in love with someone else, she presented him with a special shirt. This she had smeared in blood given to her by the centaur Nessus, who had told her the blood was a potion that would keep her marriage strong. In fact, the blood in the shirt began to burn through Hercules's flesh. In agony, he rampaged across the land, tearing up trees. But, realizing that there would be no release from the pain, he built his own funeral pyre, spread out his lion's mane, and lay down to die.

▶ Hercules and Deinaeira were traveling together when they came to a river. Hercules swam across, but the water was too fast-flowing for Deinaeira. The centaur Nessus, however, often ferried people across and began to carry Deinaeira. But Nessus was so overcome by Deinaeira's beauty that he fell in love with her and tried to carry her away. To stop Nessus, Hercules shot an arrow dipped in the Hydra's gall, killing the centaur. As Nessus died, he took vengeance on Hercules: He gave Deinaeira a vial of his own poisonous blood, but told her that it was a love charm.

Where in the sky?

Hercules is a large, scattered, and not very bright constellation in the northern sky. It reaches its highest point in June. In the middle of Hercules's head is the star Ras Algethi, which is one of the largest stars known. It is 600 times larger than the diameter of the Sun.

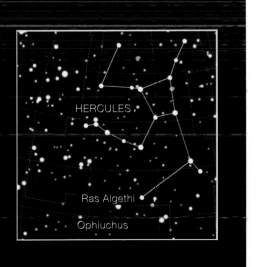

Did you know?

● In the constellations, Hercules is usually shown kneeling down. This is perhaps because Hercules was the Greek version of the earlier Sumerian hero Gilgamesh. Gilgamesh was often shown in a similar position with his foot resting on the beast he had just slain.

● Although Hercules's father was the god Zeus, his mother was not Zeus's wife, the goddess Hera, but a mortal. Hera punished Zeus's love affair by driving Hercules insane for a short time. During this period Hercules killed his first wife and three sons. To overcome his guilt at the killings, he was set Twelve Labors to complete.

● Realizing that Hercules was dying from the poisoned shirt that she had given him, Deinaeira killed herself.

● When Hercules was in agony, he threw his servant Lichas into the sea, where he turned to stone and became Mount Lichada on the Greek island of Euboea.

Hydra

As a giant serpent, it is appropriate that the Hydra is the largest and longest constellation, stretching almost a quarter of the way around the northern sky. From Cancer to Libra, Hydra is so long that it can take more than six hours to rise. It was believed that the Hydra was the offspring of the monster giant Typhon and the half-woman, half-serpent Echidna. This made Hydra a sibling to Ladon the dragon, who is represented in the constellations as Draco. Cutting the head off the Hydra was the second of Hercules's Twelve Labors. After he did this, Hercules extracted poison from the Hydra's gall and used it to kill a dozen enemies. Unfortunately, this poison was also ultimately used to kill Hercules himself.

▶ Before entering the swamp where the Hydra lived, Hercules covered his mouth and nose with a cloth to stop himself from breathing in the poisonous fumes. He fired flaming arrows into the Hydra's lair to provoke the Hydra into attacking him. But each time Hercules cut off one of the Hydra's heads, two would grow in its place. Luckily, Hercules's charioteer Iolaus came to help. Holding burning branches, Iolaus burned the stumps where Hercules had just cut off the Hydra's heads. This stopped new heads growing. With all the heads cut off, Hercules made his arrows poisonous by dipping them in the creature's gall.

Where in the sky?

Hydra's most distinctive feature is the group of six stars at the head of the snake. In the Northern Hemisphere, Hydra appears low in the sky, with its head reaching its highest point at midnight on January 31, but its tail reaching its highest point in April.

Did you know?

● In the sky, Hydra's head is south of Cancer the Crab, which Hera had sent to help fight Hercules. The crab bit Hercules, who then stamped on it.

● Hydra's middle head was immortal. Only with Iolaus's help could Hercules reach it. Once he had cut it off, Hercules buried it under a heavy rock.

● Although successful, Hercules's slaying of the Hydra would be disqualified as one of his Twelve Labors because he had been helped by Iolaus. He would have to complete an additional task.

● On the back of the constellation of the Hydra appear the constellations Corvus the Crow and Crater the Cup. Some myths link the Hydra with the water snake in the story of the Crater and why the Crow was punished by Apollo.

Leo

The fifth constellation in the Zodiac is Leo, the Lion. The shape of a crouching lion can be clearly seen in a constellation that dominates spring nights in the Northern Hemisphere and fall nights in the Southern Hemisphere. In the first of Hercules's Twelve Labors, the hero was set the task of skinning the ferocious Nemean Lion, whose pelt couldn't be cut by any metal or stone. Before the encounter, Hercules stayed with a poor man, Molorchos, whose son had been killed by the lion. Molorchos advised Hercules not to attack the lion with his club, but to wrestle it. Molorchos also told him that the lion's cave had two exits, so to trap the lion, Hercules would first have to block off one of the exits.

► Hercules proved himself strong enough to move a boulder to block one of the exits to the lion's cave and trap it inside. He was also strong enough to wrestle with the lion, and even strong enough to choke it to death. But how was he going to skin it? If no metal or stone could cut the lion's pelt, and if Hercules himself wasn't strong enough to cut into it, what was the only thing left? The lion itself. Hercules used the lion's own sharp claws to skin it. Once he had skinned the animal, Hercules wore its pelt as a cloak and its head as a helmet.

Where in the sky?

Leo is the easiest constellation in the Zodiac to recognize. It lies south of the north-pointing stars Merak and Dubhe in the Big Dipper. Its head and mane are like a question mark, with its brightest star, Alpha Leonis, at the base.

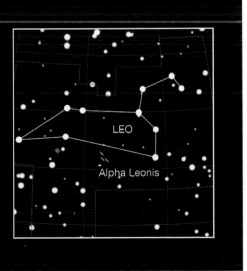

LEO

Alpha Leonis

Did you know?

● Meteor showers called the Leonids can be seen in Leo around November 16 in the northern skies. In ancient Greece and Rome, the Leonids were thought of as messengers or angels sent from the heavens.

● Five thousand years ago, at midday on the summer solstice—the longest day of the year in the Northern Hemisphere (around June 22)—the Sun passed through the constellation Leo. From this Leo became associated with high summer and the Sun. Leo has often been shown surrounded by the Sun's rays.

● Why do many fountains show water coming out of lions' mouths? The link between Leo and fresh water might originally have been made in ancient Egypt when the River Nile flooded while the Sun was in Leo.

Lepus

In Greek mythology, there are two stories about Lepus the hare. The first is the tale of why the hare was placed among the constellations, while the second explains the hare's movement across the night sky. The first story tells how there were no hares on the Greek island of Leros until a man brought in a pregnant female. Soon everyone began raising hares, but the hares quickly overran the island, eating and ruining all the crops. The population was close to starvation when the people managed to work together to drive the hares off the island. The image of the hare was placed among the constellations as a warning that one can very easily have too much of a good thing.

▶ According to some Greek myths, Canis Major, the greater dog, is the hound of Orion the Hunter. Orion's dog chases Lepus the hare through the night sky but never catches up with it. Finally, the constellation Lepus sets, followed by Canis Major. But the following evening, Lepus will appear again and later on Canis Major will also emerge to resume his never-ending chase. A similar story illustrates the saying that hares hate the sound of birds. This can also be witnessed in the night skies, where Lepus sets as Corvus the Crow rises.

Where in the sky?

Lepus is found at the feet of the giant Orion. The hunter's dog, Canis Major, lies immediately to the east, ready to pounce. Lepus reaches its highest point in mid-December. Lying south of the Equator, it is visible all over the world outside the Arctic Circle.

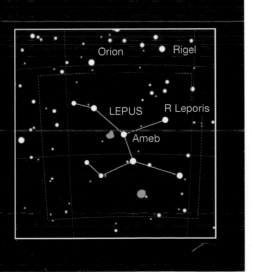

Did you know?

● In some versions of the Lepus story, it is Hermes, the swift messenger god, who put the hare in the constellations because of the animal's speed.

● Arab astronomers originally saw the stars of Lepus as the throne of Orion. At other times they imagined the stars as four camels drinking water out of the Milky Way.

● In Lepus is the reddish star R Leporis, which is a variable star—a star whose brightness seems to change. When it is dimmer, it is a deeper red. R Leporis isn't shown in the main constellation stars, but it is just beyond the hare's face.

● In both Chinese and Aztec mythology, there is a story of a rabbit on the Moon. This comes from seeing the shape of a rabbit in the seas of the Moon. In Europe and North America, it was more common to picture the face of a man in the Moon.

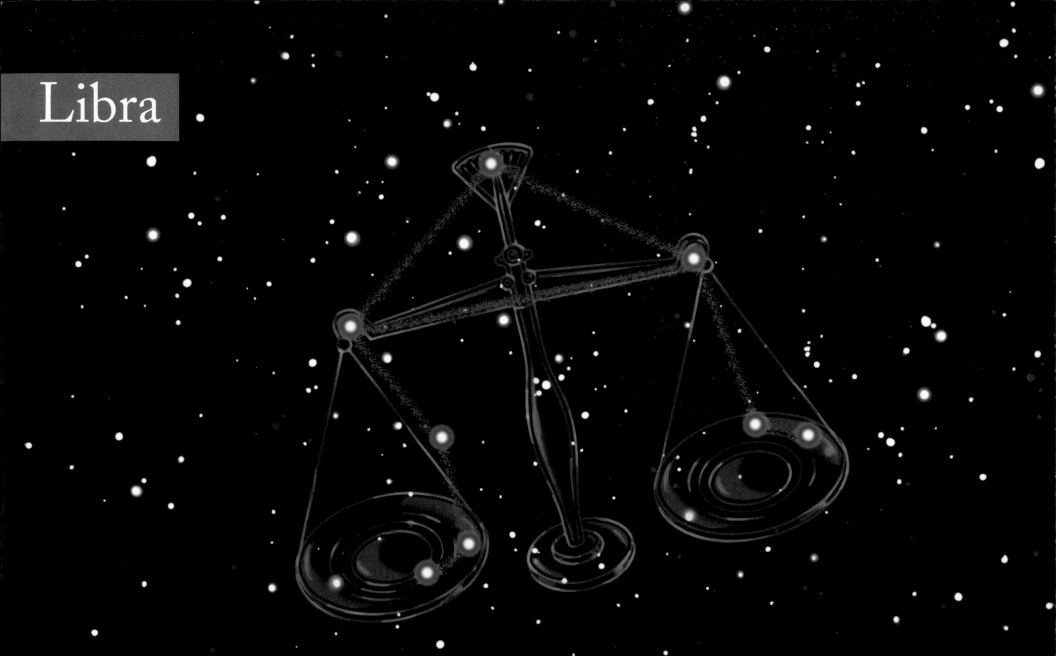

Libra

Libra, whose scales represent balance, is the only constellation of the Zodiac that isn't an animal. Two thousand years ago, the Sun would have passed through Libra in September, when the days in the Northern Hemisphere were of equal length to those in the Southern Hemisphere—that is, it was a time when the hemispheres themselves were balanced. Although to the ancient Greeks, Libra was just the claws of the older, larger constellation Scorpius, the Romans recognized Libra as a separate constellation. They connected the scales of Libra with Virgo, the constellation beside it, who was seen as Astraea, the goddess of justice. Thus, the idea of the scales of justice was linked to Libra.

▶ During the Golden Age, Astraea lived as an immortal on Earth. This was a time when crops grew all year without needing to be farmed, when there was no disease, when people didn't wage war, and when they didn't age. But people grew greedy, they began to fight among themselves, and the year was divided into four seasons. Appalled at the injustices that she saw, Astraea became a hermit in the hills. But the behavior of people only worsened and so Astraea abandoned humankind altogether, flying up into the heavens to become the constellation Virgo, with her scales as Libra.

Where in the sky?

Libra lies between Virgo to the west and Scorpius to the east. It is best seen by extending Scorpius's pincers to form a huge pair of claws. It is visible everywhere outside the Arctic Circle. It reaches its highest point in early May.

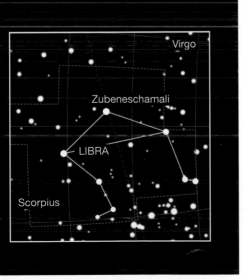

Did you know?

● Libra's star Zubeneschamali is the only star that we can spot with our eyes that shines with a greenish light.

● In ancient Rome, the libra, which means "scales," was the unit of measurement for one pound in weight (329 grams). It was abbreviated to "lb" and that abbreviation is still used today when we refer to a pound in weight.

● The scales as a symbol of justice existed in ancient Egyptian mythology. After a person died, it was believed that they passed to the Underworld, where Anubis, the jackal-headed god, weighed their hearts. If the weight was the same as a feather, the person was pure, but if the heart weighed more than or less than a feather, then the person was impure and his or her heart was eaten.

Little Bear

As long ago as 600 BCE, sailors used the Little Bear to help them navigate. At the end of its tail is the North Star, or Polaris, the most northerly star in the night sky. As the North Star moves very little and is always near north, it is a very reliable marker. Once sailors understood where north was, they could begin to work out other stars and constellations and the route that they needed to take. The seven stars in Little Bear form a pattern like a reversed Big Dipper. Indeed, the Little Bear is sometimes called the Little Dipper. One version of its myth states that the constellation is a dog, which might explain its long tail. After all, bears don't have long tails, do they?

► Zeus was the son of the Titans Cronos and Rhea, but it had been prophesied that Cronos would be overthrown by one of his children. To avoid this, Cronos swallowed all his sons and daughters as soon as they had been born. When Rhea was pregnant with Zeus, she escaped to the island of Crete, where she gave birth and left Zeus in the care of two nymphs, Adrasteia and Ida. According to one myth, when he grew up, Zeus rewarded the nymphs' good work by placing them in the heavens, with Ida as the Little Bear and Adrasteia as the Great Bear.

Where in the sky?

Take the two stars farthest from the handle in the Big Dipper's bowl. Draw a line from the base one (Merak) to the star at the rim (Dubhe) and continue straight until you reach the North Star—you've found the Little Bear's tail.

Did you know?

● After leaving Zeus in Crete, Rhea tricked Cronos by giving him a large stone wrapped in swaddling clothes to eat and telling him that it was Zeus. When Zeus grew up, he forced his father to regurgitate all of Zeus's older brothers and sisters, before banishing Cronos to Tartarus, the land beneath the surface of the Earth.

● The Ursids are the Little Bear's largest meteor shower and are best seen between December 18 and 25. They appear near the star Kochab, which is the one by the bear's right ear.

● Other interpretations of the Little Bear say that when Callisto was made into the constellation the Great Bear, her son Arcas became Little Bear and not Boötes.

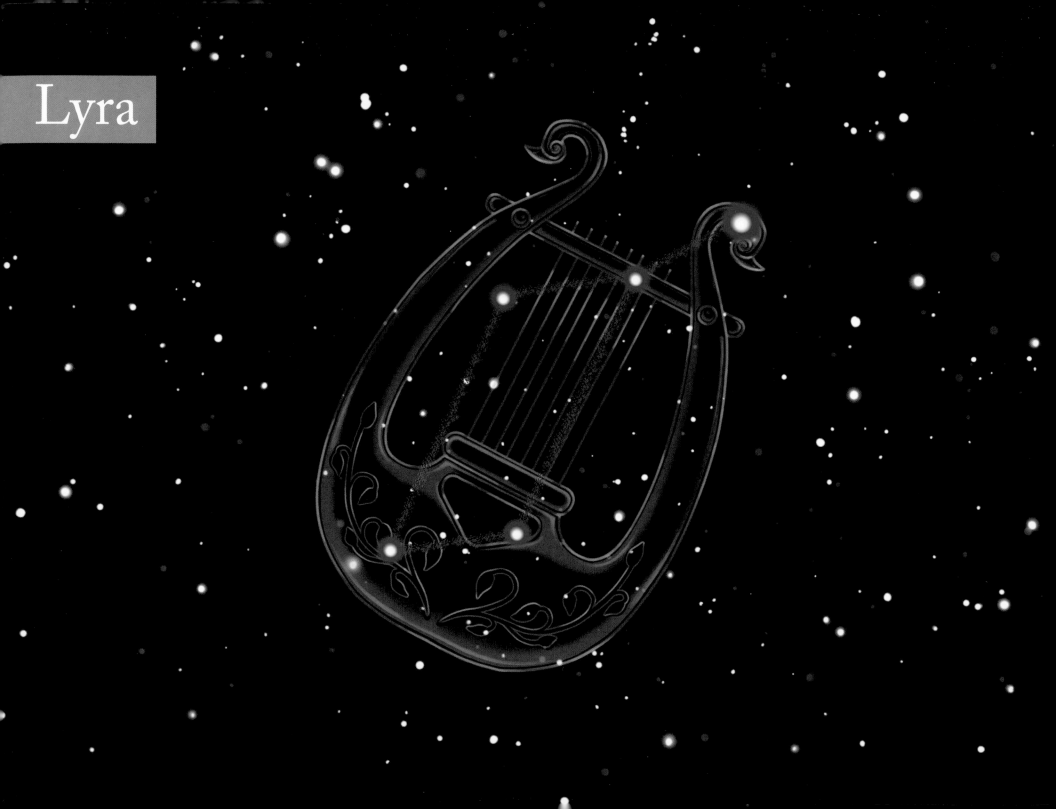

Lyra

The god Hermes invented the musical instrument the lyre out of a tortoise shell. Apollo gave it to Orpheus, the greatest singer in antiquity, who could charm animals and even trees with his music. But when his wife, the nymph Eurydice, was bitten by a viper and died, Orpheus was so distraught that he stopped singing and no longer played his lyre. He was in such despair that he risked his own life in going to the Underworld in the hope that he could bring Eurydice back from the dead. Playing his music again, he managed to charm Charon, the deathly boatman who carried souls across the River Styx, and he calmed the wild dog Cerberus, who let him pass into the Underworld.

▶ Hades, the king of the Underworld, granted Orpheus's wish to return Eurydice to the land of the living. But there was one condition: Eurydice would follow Orpheus and he wasn't allowed to turn around to look at her until they were both completely back among the living. Orpheus began his long journey, having to trust that Eurydice was following him. But as he reached the light, he couldn't resist the temptation any longer and turned to see if his wife was really there. As he did so, he heard her cry and saw Eurydice dragged back to the Underworld forever.

Where in the sky?

Lyra is easy to spot on the western edge of the Milky Way. It includes Vega, the fifth brightest star in the heavens. Lyra is best seen in the Northern Hemisphere and down to the Tropics, but farther south it begins to disappear from view.

Did you know?

● After Eurydice was lost, Orpheus rejected the love of other women, who then began throwing rocks and spears at him. At first his music was able to charm the weapons to fall beside him, but the women made so much noise that they eventually drowned out the sound of the music, and the weapons began wounding Orpheus. He was killed and his lyre was placed in the heavens.

● After Orpheus's death, his head floated downstream, still calling out his wife's name.

● Vega is the second brightest star in the Northern Hemisphere. Many star names are related to the story behind their constellation, but Vega comes from the Arabic for "swooping vulture." This is because Arab astronomers didn't see a lyre in the constellation but a bird.

Ophiuchus

Ophiuchus (pronounced Off-ee-YOO-cuss) is the Serpent Holder, but he is identified as Asclepius the healer in Greek mythology. So what links serpents and snakes with healing? Perhaps it is because each year a snake sheds its skin and seems to be reborn, in the same way that someone can become ill and appear old but then recover and look youthful again. There is also the case of Glaucus, the son of King Minos of Crete, who fell into a huge vase of honey and drowned. After Asclepius saw a snake heal another snake with an herb, he used the herb on Glaucus, who recovered. Today the international symbol of medicine is a staff with a snake (sometimes two) twined around it.

▶ Asclepius was taught medicine by the centaur Chiron. By the time Asclepius was an adult he could heal all kinds of ailments, even helping people who seemed to be near death. To most people, this would make Asclepius a hero, but not to Hades, god of the Underworld, who saw his realm threatened by the great healer. Hades protested to Zeus, who threw a thunderbolt at Asclepius, striking him dead. Now the stream of dead bodies to Hades would flow again. But seeing Apollo, Asclepius's father, so upset, Zeus placed Asclepius in the heavens as Ophiuchus.

Where in the sky?

North of Scorpius, Ophiuchus reaches its highest point in early June. Situated over the Equator, it is fully visible in the northern summer and southern winter, although not at northern and southern extremes.

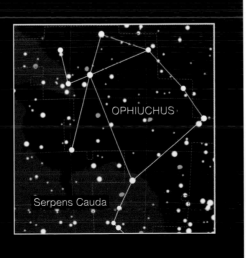

OPHIUCHUS

Serpens Cauda

Did you know?

● Apollo was so upset after his son's death that he killed the three Cyclopes, the one-eyed giants who made Zeus's thunderbolts.

● Ophiuchus and the serpent he is holding were once seen as the same constellation, but today the serpent is a separate constellation, Serpens.

● We know that there are 12 constellations in the Zodiac—the path that the Sun takes through the skies—but the Sun also passes through Ophiuchus's feet. In fact, the Sun spends longer passing through Ophiuchus than it does through Scorpius. Some people think that Ophiuchus ought to be the 13th constellation in the Zodiac.

● Ophiuchus is located between Aquila, Serpens, and Hercules.

Orion

One of the best-known constellations, Orion appears in different stories all around the world. In the constellation, the ancient Sumerians imagined their hero Gilgamesh fighting the bull of Heaven, which is perhaps why Orion appears facing Taurus the bull in the night sky. To the Jews, Orion represented biblical Samson. The Chimu Indians, who lived in what is now Peru, saw the three stars of Orion's belt as a criminal held by the arms, with the four stars outlining Orion as vultures about to tear him apart. Some Brazilian tribes imagined Orion as part of a larger constellation of a caiman. To the Inuits in the Arctic, Orion's star Betelgeuse was a bear and the three stars of Orion's belt were hunters.

▶ To the ancient Greeks, Orion was a giant hunter. He attempted to charm Merope, King Oenopion's daughter, into falling in love with him, and when he failed, he tried to force her to kiss him. In punishment, Oenopion blinded him. Without his sight, Orion found his way to the forge of Hephaestus, the god of blacksmiths. Taking pity on Orion, Hephaestus offered his assistant Cedalion to act as his eyes. Orion put the youth on his shoulders and, because an oracle had told him that the Sun would restore his sight, he walked east toward the sunrise. As the Sun's rays fell on Orion, he found that he could see again.

Where in the sky?

The seven brightest stars of Orion form an hourglass shape, or an "H" pinched in the middle. Orion lies partly on the Milky Way. It has three bright stars on its belt, as well as Betelgeuse, a supergiant star, on its right shoulder.

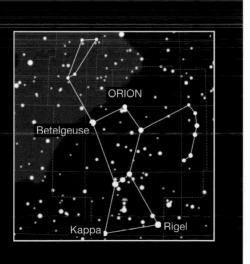

ORION

Betelgeuse

Kappa   Rigel

Did you know?

● In ancient Egypt, the constellation Orion represented Osiris, god of the Underworld, who was killed and torn apart by his brother Set. His wife, Isis, reassembled the body, at which point Osiris became immortal and ascended to the sky. Isis, seen in the star Sirius in neighboring constellation Canis Major, follows Osiris across the night sky.

● It has been suggested that the positioning of the pyramids of Giza in Egypt follow the pattern of the stars in Orion, and that the Great Pyramid, in which the Pharaoh Khufu is buried, was an imagined gateway between Osiris in the heavens and the Pharaoh's body on Earth.

● Orion is at its highest at midnight in mid-December, when it is fully visible from all places except Arctic and Antarctic regions.

● Rigel, the bottom right star by Orion's left foot, is the seventh brightest star in the sky.

Pegasus

Pegasus is a winged horse. However, its wings don't appear in its constellation, as only the front half of the horse is shown. He is mostly connected to the story of the hero Bellerophon. Guilty of murder, Bellerophon was sent as punishment to work for King Proetus. The King forgave Bellerophon, but the king's wife, Anteia, fell in love with him. When Bellerophon rejected her affections, she told the king that he had attacked her. Not wanting to execute Bellerophon, Proetus sent him away to his father-in-law, Iobates, asking him to find a way for Bellerophon to die. Iobates also didn't want to execute Bellerophon, but reluctantly set him on a mission that would probably kill him—slaying the fire-breathing Chimaera monster.

▶ Pegasus was drinking at a spring when the hero Bellerophon tamed the horse with a golden bridle. With Pegasus under his control, Bellerophon rode off into the sky in search of the Chimaera. On finding the Chimaera, Bellerophon swooped down, firing arrows and attacking with his lance, until he had killed the monster. After other adventures together, Bellerophon became arrogant and, still riding Pegasus, tried to fly up Mount Olympus to join the gods. But before he reached the top, Bellerophon fell back down to Earth, while Pegasus continued rising into the heavens. Bellerophon survived the fall, but spent his remaining years as a blind, crippled hermit.

Where in the sky?

Pegasus is a member of the Andromeda group of constellations and overlaps with her: Andromeda's head makes up part of Pegasus's body. In the constellation, the body of the horse is known as the Great Square. Pegasus reaches its highest point at midnight in September.

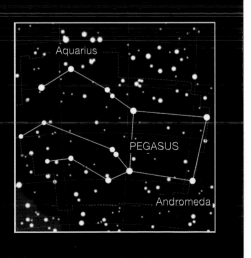

Did you know?

● The name Pegasus comes from the Greek meaning "water springs." When Pegasus stamped his hoof on Mount Helicon, a fountain was formed.

● After his time with Bellerophon, Pegasus worked for Zeus carrying his thunder and lightning for him.

● According to one version of the myth, the Chimaera had the front of a lion, the tail of a snake, and the body of a goat. Other versions describe it as having three heads: one like a lion, one like a goat, and another like a dragon.

● Some versions say that Perseus, instead of using winged slippers, rode Pegasus when he rescued Andromeda.

● When Perseus cut off the Gorgon Medusa's head, Pegasus sprang out of her body.

Perseus

Although Perseus is part of Andromeda's story, he is best known for his encounter with the Gorgon Medusa. When King Polydectes wanted to be rid of Perseus, he set the young man on an impossible mission: to bring back the head of Medusa, whose gaze turned every living creature to stone. Polydectes may have hoped that Perseus would never return from his journey, but the king hadn't considered that Perseus was the son of Zeus and was supported by the gods. Before beginning his mission, Perseus was given a bronze shield by the goddess Athena, a sword made out of diamond by Hephaestus, winged sandals that allowed him to fly by Hermes, and a helmet from Hades that made him invisible.

▶ When Perseus saw the first human figure that had been turned to stone, he knew that he had reached Medusa's lair and that he must put on his helmet of invisibility. From there he moved forward through the trail of men and animals who had been turned to stone, only looking at the reflection in his shield to find his way to Medusa. Reaching the sleeping Gorgon, Perseus cut off her head. Without looking it in the eye, he picked up the head by its hair of snakes and put it in a bag. Returning to Polydectes, Perseus pulled out Medusa's head and the king was turned to stone.

Where in the sky?

Perseus is in the Northern Hemisphere near other constellations from the Andromeda Group. Found partly on the Milky Way, it lies between Cassiopeia and Taurus. It reaches its highest point in November and is best seen in northern winter skies.

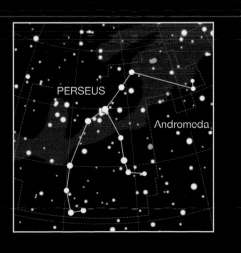

PERSEUS

Andromeda

Did you know?

● Perseus's mother had been banished by her father, Acrisius, when a prophecy had predicted that Acrisius would be killed by his grandson. Years later when Perseus was at an athletic contest, he threw a discus that accidentally killed Acrisius. The prophecy had come true.

● Before Perseus reached Medusa, he first had to pass the Graeae, three of Medusa's sisters who acted as lookouts. But as they only had one eye among them, and handed it to each other in turn, Perseus was quickly able to snatch it from them and throw it into a lake. Then he easily passed the Graeae.

● After Perseus had defeated Polydectes, the goddess Athena set Medusa's head in the middle of her shield.

● The most striking meteor shower of the year, the Perseids, appears in Perseus in August.

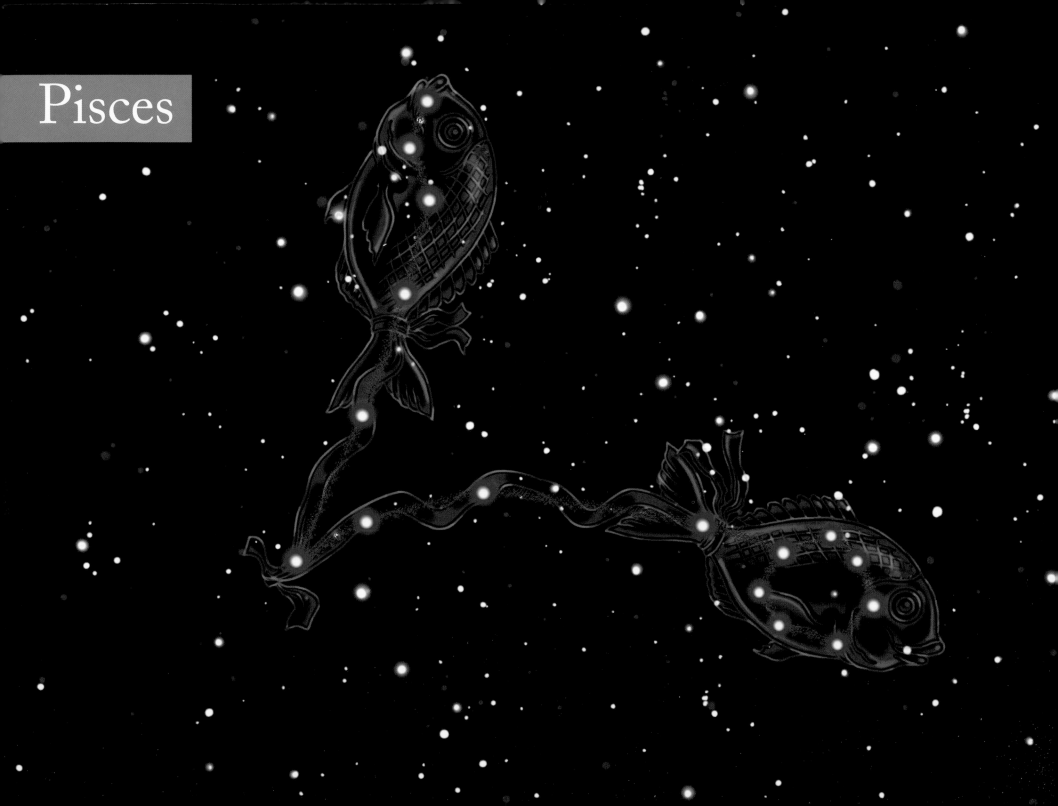

Pisces

We read that Zeus is the king of the gods, but how did he come to be king? In the ancient Greek myths of how the world was created, Zeus and his group of gods, the Olympians, were at war against other groups of gods, the Titans and the Giants. After a great battle, the Olympian gods defeated the Titans and the Giants, and Mother Earth was banished to Tartarus, the Underworld. Would Zeus now become king of the gods? Not quite. In the Underworld, Mother Earth produced a new weapon: Typhon, the most monstrous, fire-breathing giant with a hundred dragons' heads and a body tall enough to reach the sky. The battle between the Olympians and the Titans and Giants was not yet over.

▶ Mother Earth sent Typhon to attack the Olympian gods. Aphrodite, goddess of love, and her son Eros, god of love, hid among the reeds on the banks of the River Euphrates. When the wind rustled through the bulrushes, Aphrodite feared that Typhon was approaching and, with her son, leapt into the water, where they were both turned into fish. In an alternative story, an egg fell into the water, and two fish rolled it ashore. On land, doves sat on the egg until Aphrodite hatched from it. Out of gratitude to the two fish, she placed them in the constellations as Pisces.

Where in the sky?

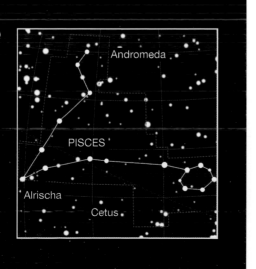

Pisces lies between Aquarius to the west and Aries to the east. Its stars are faint. The head of the northward-pointing fish is pointing at Andromeda. The star where the two fish are connected is Alrischa, a double star.

Did you know?

● The goat Pan alerted the other gods of Typhon's approach before diving into a river and becoming the goat-fish Capricornus.

● In the constellation Pisces, the fish are pictured joined at the tail but swimming away from one another. Some say that Aphrodite and Eros tied themselves together by rope so as not to be separated when they jumped into the river.

● Pisces is the plural for fish in Latin.

● The spring equinox, when the Earth's tilt toward the Sun is equally in favor of the Northern and Southern Hemispheres, happens when the Sun appears to pass the stars that make up Pisces. At noon on the day of the equinox, the Sun is directly over the Equator.

Sagittarius

If you find Sagittarius in the night sky, you are looking toward the center of the Milky Way, the galaxy that contains our Solar System. The Milky Way is shaped like a disk, but because we are looking at it from the inside, it appears to us like a ribbon. One of the constellations of the Zodiac, Sagittarius is an archer, although different civilizations have told varied stories about his character. To the Romans he was identified as the gentle, educated centaur Chiron, while to the Sumerians he was the god of war. According to Greek mythology, he was Crotus, the inventor of archery, who lived among the nine muses—the goddesses who inspired literature, science, music, and dancing.

▶ As a satyr, Crotus had the upper body of a man but the legs of a goat. He became well known for his skill and speed as a hunter on horseback through the woods, but he was also a good musician. As a reward for his friendship, the Muses asked Zeus to represent him in the constellations. Zeus wanted to show all Crotus's skills in one body: He gave him the legs of a horse because he rode a great deal, and he added arrows, because these would show both Crotus's accuracy and his swiftness.

Where in the sky?

Sagittarius lies between Ophiuchus to the west and Capricornus to the east. It is best seen in the Southern Hemisphere and is at its highest in June and July. In the more northern parts of the Northern Hemisphere it sits low on the horizon.

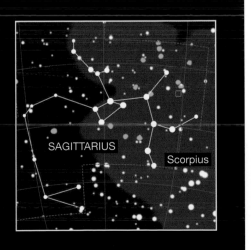

SAGITTARIUS

Scorpius

Did you know?

● The word "Sagittarius" comes from "sagita," which is Latin for "arrow."

● The Sun shines in front of Sagittarius on the December solstice, the shortest day of the year in the Northern Hemisphere, which falls on or near December 21.

● Sagittarius also includes an asterism called the Teapot. The Teapot is best seen in the Northern Hemisphere in late summer and early fall skies.

● As Sagittarius is in such a dense part of the Milky Way, it contains many clusters and nebulae, which are clouds of dust, hydrogen, helium, and other gases.

● After studying the planet Pluto, the space probe New Horizons will explore space in the direction of Sagittarius. But it will take thousands of years to reach the constellation, by which time the probe's batteries will be dead.

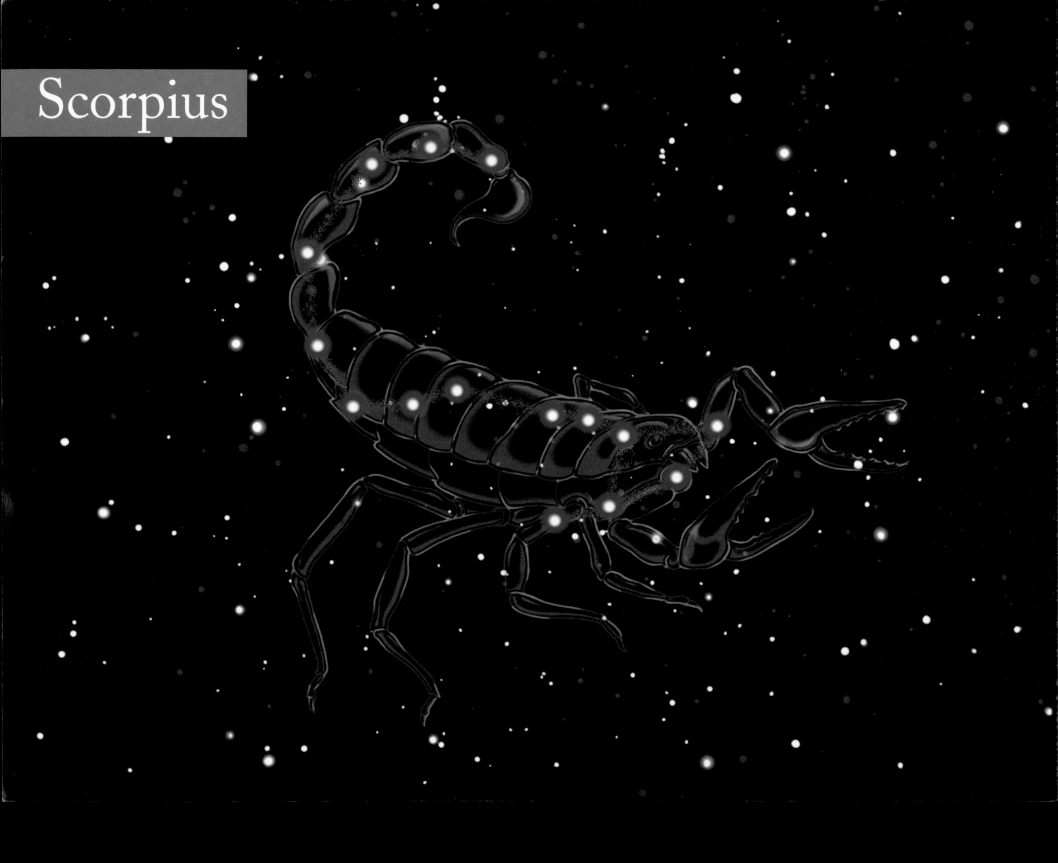

Scorpius

Part of the Zodiac, Scorpius is unusual in that it actually looks like the animal it is named after—you can clearly see the curl of the scorpion's tail. But Scorpius hasn't always looked the way it does today. The ancient Greek constellation for Scorpius was larger until the 1st century BCE, when the Romans separated its claws and from them created a separate constellation for Libra. Picturing a scorpion in the constellation, however, is even older than the ancient Greeks: the Sumerians, in what would today be Iraq, saw a scorpion in their skies 5,000 years ago. There are different stories about the scorpion, but in both Greek myths it stings Orion because he has become arrogant.

▶ In one story Orion boasted that he could kill any wild beast. To prove Orion wrong and as a punishment, the scorpion was sent to kill him. But after Orion was killed, Asclepius the healer treated his wounds and Orion rose again. This story is shown in the movement of the constellations: As Scorpius rises in the east, Orion sets in the west, but the following night Orion will rise again. In another version of the encounter between Orion and the scorpion, Orion threw himself upon Artemis, the goddess of hunting. Insulted by Orion's behavior, Artemis sent the scorpion to sting him.

Where in the sky?

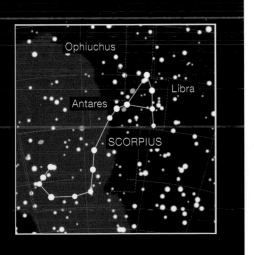

Scorpius lies across the Milky Way, with Ophiuchus to the north. Stretching a long way south of the path of the Sun, Scorpius is easily seen at the Equator and in the Southern Hemisphere. It reaches its highest point at midnight in June.

Did you know?

● In Egypt, the stars of Scorpius were once seen as a serpent, while among the Maori people of New Zealand, Scorpius represented a fishhook. In their myth, the hero Maui was fishing when he pulled out of the ocean a piece of land, which was New Zealand. The hook broke free from the land with such force that it flew right up into the sky, where it has remained ever since.

● The brightest star in Scorpius is Antares, which is several hundred times larger than our Sun. Antares's name comes from the Greek for "rival of Mars." This is because Antares has a reddish-orange color like the planet Mars.

● In Hawaii, the constellation of Scorpius is seen as the fishhook of the demigod Maui.

Taurus

One of the constellations of the Zodiac, Taurus has been linked with a bull or cow for more than 7,000 years. In ancient Egyptian culture, Osiris was shown as a bull-god and identified with the constellation. In one of the earliest works of literature, the Sumerian *Epic of Gilgamesh*, the goddess Ishtar sends Taurus the bull to kill Gilgamesh. In the sky, only the front half of the bull can be seen, with the reddish star Aldebaran marking the bull's bloodshot eye and its long horn extending upward to two bright stars. The constellation also includes two beautiful clusters that can be seen by the naked eye: the Pleiades on its back and the Hyades, which mark its face.

▶ Princess Europa was playing by the seashore when Zeus looked down from the heavens and noticed how lovely she was. Telling his son Hermes to drive the king's cattle down to the shore, Zeus changed himself into a bull and moved unsuspected among the animals. With a coat as white as snow and horns like polished metal, he was the finest-looking bull and charmed Europa. When he crouched down, she climbed onto his back. But then he quickly carried Europa out to sea and she was forced to cling on until they had reached the island of Crete.

Where in the sky?

The main part of Taurus is visible all around the world. Lying northwest of Orion, in the Northern Hemisphere it is best seen in the winter skies. It is quickly identifiable by the redness of its star Aldebaran.

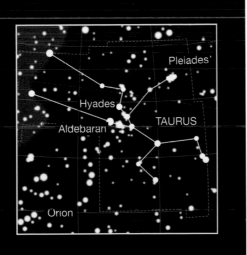

Did you know?

● The Pleiades (PLEE-a-dees) cluster of stars is only 50 million years old, which is very young in terms of the Universe. A cluster is a group of up to a few thousand stars that were formed by the same giant molecular cloud.

● To the Iroquois of North America, the seven stars of the Pleiades were seven young boys doing a war dance. To the Aztecs in Mexico, the Hyades cluster was an ox's jawbone.

● To the early Hebrews, Taurus was the first constellation in their Zodiac and was represented by the first letter in their alphabet, Aleph.

● In Persian mythology, the constellation represents the bull Mithras, the god who combines the purity and invincibility of the Sun with a warrior spirit.

Virgo

The largest constellation in the Zodiac, Virgo is also the only woman. Rising in the sky in the spring, the constellation is associated with the fertility of new crops and with women. One Greek story about the creation of the seasons sees Virgo as Persephone, daughter of Demeter, the goddess of corn. In the fields one day, Persephone was kidnapped by Hades and taken to the Underworld. Having lost her daughter, Demeter cursed the fields so that the crops failed. When she learned where Persephone was, Demeter confronted Zeus, who could only permit the girl to return to her mother for six months of each year. This represented spring and summer when the crops grow, while her time in the Underworld represented autumn and winter.

▶ In another story, the god of wine, Dionysus, taught Icarius how to grow grape vines and make wine. One day, he offered his new drink to local shepherds. They enjoyed the wine, but when they became drunk, their friends didn't understand what had happened to them and thought that Icarius had poisoned them. Acting in what they thought was revenge, the shepherds' friends killed Icarius. His daughter, Erigone, was unable to carry on living without her father and she hanged herself from the tree beneath which his body lay. Dionysus then placed her in the heavens as the constellation Virgo.

Where in the sky?

Virgo is best found by its brightest star, Spica, which in the Northern Hemisphere is most easily seen on spring and early summer evenings. To find Virgo, extend the curve of the Big Dipper to Arcturus and continue the curve until you reach Spica.

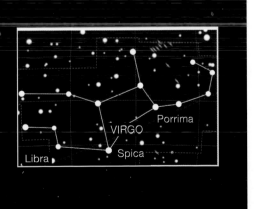

Did you know?

● Unable to find Persephone, Demeter had asked the Great Bear what he had seen, because he was a constellation that never set. But since Persephone had been kidnapped during the day, the Great Bear told her to ask the Sun, who informed Demeter that Persephone was in the Underworld.

● According to some myths, Maera, Icarius's dog, was placed in the heavens as Canis Minor, while Icarius became the constellation Boötes.

● Virgo's brightest star Spica is located in the constellation in the ear of wheat that she is holding. Spica is around 260 light years away.

● Porrima, the star between Virgo's left elbow and her body, is, in fact, a pair of stars orbiting one another every 169 years.

The Milky Way

The Milky Way is the galaxy that contains nine-tenths of all visible stars. In one of its swirling spiral arms is our Solar System and in that is Earth. The Sun, too, is in the Milky Way, about two-thirds of the way from the center to the outer edge. The Milky Way is approximately 100,000 light years in diameter and 2,000 light years thick. Although not connected, different cultures have all seen the Milky Way as a heavenly river or road. In Hebrew tradition it is the River of Light; in India it is a reflection of the River Ganges; in ancient Egypt it was the heavenly version of the River Nile. To the Chinese, it was the Sky River, represented on Earth by the great Yellow River.

▶ Hercules was the son of Zeus and Alcmene, a mortal. The goddess Hera, Zeus's wife, was usually jealous of Zeus's children with other women and would punish both the rival and the children. But this time Zeus tricked Hera into looking after the baby. He arranged for her to find Hercules as if the baby had been abandoned. Assuming the baby was hungry, Hera began to breastfeed him, which gave Hercules the gift of immortality. But then Hercules pulled too hard on her nipple and she cried out in pain. When Hera pushed the baby away from her, some of her milk flew into the sky, creating the Milky Way.

Where in the sky?

On a clear, moonless night, you might be able to spot a hazy band of starlight stretching across the sky in a large arc. It looks cloudy because it is the mixed light of thousands of stars that make up the Milky Way.

Did you know?

● According to Greek myth, the milk that didn't become the Milky Way fell to Earth and became lilies.

● The Romans believed that souls went to heaven along the Milky Way.

● The Milky Way holds about 400 billion stars. Other stars you can see that are outside the Milky Way are outside the spiral disk of the galaxy.

● All the stars in our galaxy, including the Sun, rotate around the center of the Milky Way, but even traveling at 135 miles per second (220 km/s), it takes the Sun 240 million years to complete an orbit.

● In 1610, the Italian astronomer Galileo Galilei, using a telescope, first separated the band of light of the Milky Way into individual stars.

Index